GCSE English

Dr Jekyll
& Mr Hyde

by Robert Louis Stevenson

If you're in two minds about *Dr Jekyll & Mr Hyde*, don't worry —
this CGP Workbook will help you show off your best side in the exams.

It's crammed with top-quality questions to test you on the novella's plot,
characters, themes, context and more. There's even a brilliant Exam Buster
section to help you get your essay-writing up to speed.

So trust the exam doctors at CGP to know what's best for your *Jekyll & Hyde*
grades. You'll feel like a new person by the time you've finished.

The Workbook

CONTENTS

CONTENTS

Section Four — The Writer's Techniques

Section Five — Exam Buster

Published by CGP

Editors:
Claire Boulter
Emma Cleasby
Rose Jones
Louise McEvoy
Liam Neilson
Jack Perry
Rebecca Tate

With thanks to John Sanders and Sean Walsh for the proofreading.
With thanks to Jan Greenway for the copyright research.

Acknowledgements:

Cover Illustration - Cobble stone © ROMAOSLO/iStockphoto.com

With thanks to Rex Features for permission to use the images on pages 1, 4, 15, 17 and 33.

With thanks to Nick Collinge @ Love It Studios for permission to use the images on pages 3, 7, 9, 12, 18, 27, 29 and 39.
Images from Barrow Operatic and Dramatic Society's 2014 production of 'Jekyll & Hyde'.

With thanks to Alamy for permission to use the images on pages 10, 23 and 34.

With thanks to Fotos by Failla for permission to use the images on pages 19 and 20.

With thanks to ArenaPAL for permission to use the images on pages 24 and 37.

Every effort has been made to locate copyright holders and obtain permission to reproduce sources.
For those sources where it has been difficult to trace the copyright holder of the work, we would be grateful
for information. If any copyright holder would like us to make an amendment to the acknowledgements,
please notify us and we will gladly update the book at the next reprint. Thank you.

ISBN: 978 1 78294 779 0

Printed by Elanders Ltd, Newcastle upon Tyne.

Clipart from Corel®

Based on the classic CGP style created by Richard Parsons.

How to Use this Book

Practise the four main skills you'll need for the exam

Each question tests one or more of the four skills you'll be tested on in the exam. You'll need to:

1) Write about the text in a thoughtful way, picking out appropriate examples and quotations to back up your opinions.

2) Identify and explain features of the novella's form, structure and language. Using subject terminology, show how the author uses these to create characters and settings, explore themes and affect the reader's reactions.

3) Write about the novella's context.

4) Write in a clear, well-structured and accurate way. 5% of the marks in your English Literature GCSE are for spelling, punctuation and grammar.

Most exam boards will want you write about context. Ask your teacher if you're not sure.

Use this workbook with or without the CGP Text Guide

1) This workbook is perfect to use with CGP's Text Guide for *Jekyll and Hyde*. The workbook matches each section of the Text Guide, so you can test your knowledge bit by bit.

2) You can also use this book by itself. It covers all the important parts of the text — plot, characters, context, themes and the writer's techniques.

3) The questions refer to the text in detail — you'll need a copy of the novella to make the most of the workbook.

© MGM/Kobal/REX/Shutterstock

It prepares you for the exam every step of the way

1) The exam section is jam-packed with useful advice. It guides you through how to tackle the exam, from understanding the questions to building great answers. There's also an easy-to-read mark scheme, which you can use to mark sample answers and improve answers of your own.

2) There are four pages of practice exam questions spread across the book. They give you the opportunity to use what you've revised in each section to write a realistic answer.

3) Exam tips and extra practice exam questions are included throughout the book. There are also helpful revision tasks designed to get you thinking more creatively. These are marked with stamps.

4) You can find answers to all of the questions and tasks at the back of the book.

5) Each section contains at least one 'Skills Focus' page. These pages help you to practise important skills individually. You can tackle them in any order and prioritise the skills you find the hardest.

We've brewed up some great revision questions just for you...

Now you know what the book's all about, it's time to tackle some questions. Remember, you don't have to do the sections in order — use the book in a way that works for you. Just don't sneak a look at the answers first...

Story of the Door

Mr Utterson learns about Hyde from Mr Enfield

Q1 Read the first two paragraphs of the chapter. What impression do you get of Utterson? Use a quote to support your answer.

....

....

....

Q2 'Utterson and Enfield seem to be good friends, but they have nothing in common.' Explain whether or not you agree with this statement.

....

....

Q3 Read from "**Well, it was this way**" to "**emotional as a bagpipe.**" Decide whether each statement is **true** or **false**, and find a short quote to support your answer.

a) Hyde is a man of short stature.　　　　　　　　　　　True: ☐　　False: ☐

Quote: ....

b) Hyde is weak.　　　　　　　　　　　　　　　　　　True: ☐　　False: ☐

Quote: ....

c) Enfield disliked Hyde.　　　　　　　　　　　　　　True: ☐　　False: ☐

Quote: ....

Q4 In this chapter, Enfield and Utterson discuss Jekyll but never use his name. What does this suggest?

....

....

....

Knock Knock. Who's there? Hopefully not Hyde...

In the exam, you'll need to use quotes to support your ideas if you want to get a good mark. Jot down any key quotes you find when you're working through this book — that way you'll have a list to learn.

Search for Mr Hyde

Mr Utterson reads Jekyll's will

Q1 Put these events in order by numbering the boxes. The first one has been done for you.

Dr Lanyon claims that Jekyll is "**wrong in mind**". ☐
Utterson meets Hyde for the first time. ☐
Utterson reads Jekyll's will. 1
Poole explains that the household staff must obey Hyde. ☐
Utterson describes Hyde as "**hardly human**". ☐

© Nick Collinge @ Love It Studios

Q2 Why is Utterson shocked by Jekyll's will?

....

Q3 Answer each question and then choose a quote from the text to support each answer.

a) What impression does Stevenson give of Lanyon in this chapter?

....

Quote: ....

b) How does Hyde react when he first meets Utterson?

....

Quote: ....

c) What does Utterson think Hyde will do if he finds out about Jekyll's will?

....

Quote: ....

Q4 What impression do you get of Jekyll's house? Use a quote to support your answer.

....

....

Surely there's a gag in the page title, but I just can't see it...

It's useful to think about aspects of *Jekyll and Hyde* that stay the same, as well as aspects that change. Hyde's appearance constantly unsettles other characters, which suggests that evil is part of his nature.

4

Dr Jekyll was Quite at Ease

Utterson confronts Jekyll about his friendship with Hyde

Q1 Lanyon has said that Jekyll's work involves "**scientific heresies**". What does he mean by this?

....

Q2 When Utterson mentions Hyde, a "**blackness**" appears around Jekyll's eyes. What does this suggest about Jekyll's character? Explain your answer.

....

....

Q3 Explain how this chapter gives the impression that Jekyll is hiding something.

....

....

Q4 Fill in the gaps in the passage below.

© REX/Shutterstock

By this point in the story, the reader has met all of the major characters. Apart from ...., they all act like typical .... gentlemen: they are well mannered, rational and are concerned with their .... This allows Stevenson to set up a .... between Hyde's .... and those of rest of the gentlemen.

Q5 At the end of this chapter, Utterson makes a promise to Jekyll. What is this promise?

....

 They hoped they'd see neither Hyde nor hair of Hyde...

PRACTICE TASK Explain what your opinion is of Jekyll, Hyde and Enfield so far in *Jekyll and Hyde*. You should write a couple of sentences for each character, including evidence from the text to back up your ideas.

The Carew Murder Case

Hyde murders Danvers Carew

Q1 How does Stevenson show that the attack on Carew is unprovoked?

....

....

....

Q2 Why do you think that Carew's murder is described in such vivid detail?

....

....

Q3 Compare Hyde's trampling of the young girl in 'Story of the Door' with Carew's murder. Find one quote for each event that shows how Hyde feels during the assault.

Trampling of the young girl: ....

Murder of Carew: ....

Q4 Read from "**As the cab drew up**" to "**completed his gratification.**" Decide whether each statement is **true** or **false**, and find a quote to support your answer.

a) Hyde lives in a rich area of London. **True:** ☐ **False:** ☐

Quote: ....

b) Hyde's rooms are filled with expensive items. **True:** ☐ **False:** ☐

Quote: ....

c) The inspector finds evidence that Hyde is guilty. **True:** ☐ **False:** ☐

Quote: ....

The attack on Danvers was pretty Carew-l...

In this chapter, Stevenson gives a detailed description of Victorian London. If you're writing about the setting of *Jekyll and Hyde* in the exam, you'll need to think about the context too (p.23).

 ☐   ☐   ☐

Incident of the Letter

Jekyll claims that Hyde has left forever

Q1 Read from the start of the chapter to "**in a changed voice**". What sort of atmosphere does Stevenson create in the laboratory? Explain your answer.

....

....

Q2 Answer each question and then choose a quote from the text to support each answer.

a) According to Utterson, why might Hyde have wanted to kill Jekyll?

....

Quote: ....

b) Why is Utterson worried that Carew's murder will become a scandal?

....

Quote: ....

c) Why does Jekyll show Hyde's letter to Utterson?

....

Quote: ....

Q3 Explain why Utterson is "**relieved**" by Jekyll's selfishness.

....

....

Q4 The two letters in this chapter have very similar handwriting. What does Utterson suspect has happened?

....

I letterally love writing all these puns...

Remember to consider how characters are presented at different points in the novella. In this chapter, Jekyll thinks Hyde is weak enough to be controlled, but as the story progresses, Hyde grows stronger.

Remarkable Incident of Dr Lanyon

Lanyon dies after a terrible shock

Q1 Read from the start of the chapter to **"the doctor was at peace."**
Decide whether the following statements are **true** or **false**.

	True	False
Carew was well-respected in society.	☐	☐
Utterson believes Hyde's disappearance makes up for Carew's death.	☐	☐
Jekyll has a reputation for being selfish.	☐	☐

Q2 Read from **"There at least"** to **"glad to get away."** Give two quotes from this passage which suggest that Lanyon is going to die.

Quote 1: ....

Quote 2: ....

Q3 In this chapter, how does Stevenson build on Utterson's earlier fears that Jekyll is in danger? Use a quote to support your answer.

....

....

....

Q4 At the end of the chapter, Utterson wants to read Lanyon's letter but chooses not to. What does this suggest about his character?

....

....

....

© Nick Collinge @ Love It Studios

Q5 Explain why Utterson visits Jekyll less often after the events of this chapter.

....

....

"Doctor, Doctor, I'm not feeling quite myself today..."

PRACTICE TASK

Divide a piece of paper in half. Using this chapter and Chapter Two ('Search for Mr Hyde'), create a table of quotes showing how Lanyon's appearance and behaviour change after seeing Jekyll transform.

8

Incident at the Window

Jekyll locks himself away

Q1   'Incident at the Window' is a very short chapter. What effect does this have?

....

....

Q2   Fill in the gaps in the passage below.

By this point of the story, Jekyll has lost his ability to control his .... and has

begun to fear them. This is shown by his .... before he closes the window.

The reader still doesn't know Jekyll's ...., so this event will leave them feeling

.... and ....

Q3   How has Jekyll's manner changed since 'Dr Jekyll was
Quite at Ease'? Use a quote to back up your answer.

....

....

....

Q4   How can you tell that Utterson and Enfield are shaken by what they have seen?

....

....

....

Q5   Give an example of when Stevenson uses hyperbole (exaggeration) in this chapter.

....

Jekyll looked in pane during the Incident at the Window...

The suspense surrounding Hyde and his relationship with Jekyll increases as the novella progresses.
Try not to treat each chapter in isolation — think about how different chapters build this suspense.

The Last Night

Utterson finds Hyde dead

Q1 Complete the table to show how the following features create atmosphere in the chapter.

Feature	How it creates atmosphere
The actions of Poole and the servants	
Stevenson's description of London	

Q2 Briefly explain why Poole and Utterson break into Jekyll's cabinet.

....

....

....

Q3 Hyde's death is not described in the text. What is the effect of this?

....

....

Q4 When Poole asks Utterson why he won't read Jekyll's letter, Utterson replies "**Because I fear**". What do you think Utterson fears?

....

Q5 How does Stevenson create suspense at the end of the chapter?

....

....

 Utterson and Poole, 1 — Jekyll's cabinet, 0...

There are lots of settings in the novella. Find three important quotes from the text about each of the following important settings: Jekyll's house, Hyde's house, Jekyll's laboratory and Soho.

Dr Lanyon's Narrative

Lanyon's letter reveals the truth

Q1 Why does Lanyon follow the instructions in Jekyll's letter?

....

....

Q2 What is Lanyon's impression of Hyde when he meets him? Use a quote to back up your answer.

....

....

Q3 When the potion is mixed, it changes colour and begins to smoke. What does this suggest about the potion?

....

Q4 Read from "**He put the glass to his lips**" to "**the murderer of Carew.**" Find a quote to back up each of these statements.

a) Hyde suffered during his transformation.

Quote: ....

....

b) Stevenson uses imagery to show Lanyon's horror.

Quote: ....

c) When he reflects on Hyde's transformation, Lanyon struggles to believe what he saw.

Quote: ....

Q5 Read from "**O God!**" to the end of the chapter. What effect does Lanyon's reaction to Hyde's transformation have on the reader?

....

....

Phew, that was a long letter — Lanyon's not Hastie...

Think about how Stevenson has presented Jekyll up to this point in the story. Write a short paragraph saying whether or not you sympathise with Jekyll in this chapter. Give reasons for your choice.

Henry Jekyll's Full Statement of the Case

Jekyll's letter explains everything

Q1 Put these events in order by numbering the boxes. The last one has been done for you.

Jekyll experimented on himself. ☐

Jekyll turned into Hyde without taking potion for the first time. ☐

Jekyll discovered the "**duplicity of life**". ☐

Hyde killed Danvers Carew. ☐

Jekyll requested Lanyon's help. ☐

Jekyll believed he could separate man's good and evil sides. ☐

Hyde takes poison and dies. 7

Q2 Read from the start of the chapter to "**an almost morbid sense of shame**".
Find a quote to back up each of these statements.

a) Jekyll thinks that liveliness is his greatest flaw.

Quote: ....

....

b) Jekyll claims that many people would not have considered his pleasures to be particularly bad.

Quote: ....

....

c) Jekyll liked having a good reputation.

Quote: ....

....

Q3 Why did Jekyll create the potion?

....

Q4 Jekyll writes that when he first saw Hyde in the mirror, he "**was conscious of
no repugnance, rather of a leap of welcome**". Why does Jekyll feel like this?

....

....

Jekyll loses control of Hyde and kills himself

Q1 Find quotes to back up the following statements.

a) Jekyll enjoyed being Hyde at first.

Quote: ....

b) After he stopped taking the potion, Jekyll gave in to temptation and started using it again.

Quote: ....

....

Q2 Why is it significant that Jekyll started transforming without taking the potion?

....

....

Q3 In this chapter, Jekyll describes Hyde as the "**devil**", "**the spirit of hell**" and the "**child of Hell**". What impact do these descriptions have on the reader?

....

....

Q4 What impact does the murder of Carew have on Jekyll?

....

....

....

© Nick Collinge @ Love It Studios

Q5 Jekyll claims that "**Hyde alone**" is guilty of the crimes in *Jekyll and Hyde*. Do you agree? Explain your answer.

....

....

....

My verdict — Jekyll deserves a good Hydeing...

Now you've reached the end of the novella, it's time for a recap. Make a flowchart with arrows and labels showing at least five events in Jekyll's life between his decision to invent the potion and his death.

Using Quotes

There's no point in having lots of really good opinions about the novella if you can't back them up with evidence — that's where quotes from the text come in. You won't have the text with you in the exam, so you'll need to choose some useful quotes to learn beforehand. Picking quotes isn't always easy, so here's a page to help you think about the sorts of quote you might learn and how to use them successfully in your answers. Have a go at these questions and you'll soon have cracked it.

Q1 Complete the table below to show whether each way of using quotes is good or bad. Put a tick in the relevant column.

Way of using quotes	Good	Bad
a) Writing down quotes exactly as they're written in the text		
b) Using quotes that repeat what you've just written		
c) Using quotes as part of your sentence, rather than adding them onto the end of it		
d) Including lots of long quotes		
e) Using quotes which are interesting but don't support your point		

Q2 Look at the examples and decide which use quotes well and which use them badly.

> a) Enfield and Utterson's excursions are described as the "chief jewel of each week", which implies that the men value them.
> b) Hyde's brutal nature is shown when he breaks out "in a great flame of anger, stamping with his foot, brandishing the cane, and carrying on (as the maid described it) like a madman."
> c) Utterson is deeply shocked by Hyde's appearance, regarding him with "mental perplexity".
> d) The back door of Jekyll's house is "blistered and distained", which makes it seem sinister.
> e) After Hyde disappears, Jekyll returns to society: "He came out of his seclusion".

Good quote usage: .... Bad quote usage: ....

Q3 Choose one of the examples you identified as bad in Q2 and improve it.

....

....

....

14

P.E.E.D.

Making a comment about the text is all well and good, but if you want a good mark, you'll need to explain your comment in a clear and developed way. The trick is to stick to the P.E.E.D. method. Whenever you make a **point**, back it up with an **example**, then **explain** how it supports your point. The last step is to **develop** your point by explaining the effect it has on the reader or by linking it to something else. This could be another part of the novella, a theme, or a relevant piece of context.

Q1 None of the sample answers below have used P.E.E.D. correctly. For each, say which stage of P.E.E.D. is missing, then write a sentence you could include to improve the answer.

a)
> Jekyll is shown to be under pressure to protect his reputation. In his letter, he describes how he felt a "morbid sense of shame" when he reflected on his past "irregularities". The fact that Jekyll felt such a deep sense of shame suggests that the society he was a part of would not have accepted these "irregularities", which forced Jekyll to hide part of his personality.

Missing stage: .... Addition: ....

....

....

b)
> In 'Search for Mr Hyde', Utterson is "haunted" by fantastical images of Hyde, imagining him standing by Jekyll's bed and seeing him "glide" around London. The terms "haunted" and "glide" make Hyde seem ghostly, which creates an unsettling atmosphere because it implies he is supernatural. The fact that it is Utterson who imagines these images adds to the unsettling tone of the passage. He is usually rational, so his lack of composure is disturbing.

Missing stage: .... Addition: ....

....

....

c)
> Stevenson uses Lanyon's reaction to Hyde's transformation into Jekyll to emphasise how shocking it is. Lanyon is horrified by the experience, stating that his "soul sickened" at the sight of it. Utterson and Enfield are similarly appalled when they begin to see Jekyll transform at the window, as shown by the fact that there was "horror in their eyes."

Missing stage: .... Addition: ....

....

....

Section One — Analysis of Chapters

Henry Jekyll & Edward Hyde

Q1 Find a quote from the text that suggests that Jekyll is:

a) secretive

Quote: ....

b) respected by society

Quote: ....

....

c) moral

Quote: ....

....

Q2 Briefly summarise what Jekyll believes about human nature.

....

....

....

Q3 How can you tell that Jekyll is an ambitious character?
Use a quote to back up your answer.

....

....

....

....

Q4 How does Stevenson create sympathy for Jekyll in the final
chapter of the novella? Use a quote to back up your answer.

....

....

....

Q5 Fill in the gaps in the table below. The first one has been done for you.

Event in the novella	What it reveals about Hyde
a) Hyde "**trampled**" over a young girl.	Hyde is a violent character.
b) Hyde gave the young girl's family a cheque for £100.	
c) Hyde left his home in a hurry after murdering Carew.	
d) Hyde wrote "**startling blasphemies**" on Jekyll's Bible.	

Q6 Hyde is described as "**younger**" than Jekyll. Briefly explain why you think he is younger.

....

....

Q7 Throughout the novella, many characters struggle to describe Hyde's appearance clearly. What effect does this have on the reader?

....

....

....

Q8 Find three quotes from the text which show that the other characters dislike Hyde.

1) ....

2) ....

3) ....

Q9 Throughout the story, Hyde gets taller. Why is this significant?

....

....

....

Section Two — Characters

Q10 Write a short comparison of Jekyll and Hyde's appearances. Use quotes to support your answer.

....

....

....

Q11 Jekyll claims that he "**had more than a father's interest; Hyde had more than a son's indifference**". What does this suggest about their relationship?

....

....

Q12 Explain how Jekyll's attitude to Hyde changes as the story progresses. Use a quote to support your answer.

© REX/Shutterstock

....

....

....

....

Q13 How can you tell that Hyde dislikes Jekyll?

....

....

Q14 Do you think that Jekyll and Hyde are complete opposites? Explain your answer.

....

....

....

....

Without the potion, Jekyll would get de-Hyde-rated...

PRACTICE TASK

Read 'Dr Lanyon's Narrative' from "**These particulars struck me**" to "**status in the world**", then plan an answer to the following question: **How does Stevenson present Hyde as mysterious in *Dr Jekyll and Mr Hyde?*** In your plan, you should refer to both the extract and to the novella as a whole.

Gabriel Utterson

Q1 Think of three adjectives to describe Utterson's personality, then find a short quote to back up each one.

Adjectives: ....

Quote 1: ....

Quote 2: ....

Quote 3: ....

Q2 How can you tell that Utterson is a rational character?

....

....

....

Q3 Find short quotes to back up the following statements.

a) Utterson wants to protect Jekyll's reputation after Carew's death.

Quote: ....

b) Utterson hates Hyde when he first meets him.

Quote: ....

c) After Lanyon's death, Utterson's relationship with Jekyll deteriorates.

Quote: ....

Q4 'Utterson's actions in 'The Last Night' show that he is a brave character.' Do you agree with this statement? Explain your answer.

....

....

....

Gabriel's Utter-ly obsessed with reputation...

In the exam, it's important that you can back up your arguments with examples — make sure you know a few key quotes about each major character and can explain what each one shows about them.

Dr Hastie Lanyon

Q1 Find short quotes to back up the following statements.

a) When Lanyon is introduced, he is presented as a friendly character.

Quote: ....

b) Lanyon disapproves of Jekyll's scientific experiments.

Quote: ....

c) Lanyon predicts his own death.

Quote: ....

Q2 What is Lanyon's relationship with Jekyll like? Use a quote to support your answer.

....

....

Q3 In their letters, how does Lanyon's language differ from Jekyll's? Use a quote to support your answer.

....

....

....

....

© Fotos by Failla

Q4 What causes Lanyon's death? Use a quote to back up your answer.

....

....

Hastie's top holiday destination — the Grand Lanyon...

Read 'Search for Mr Hyde' from "**The solemn butler knew and welcomed him**" to "**Since my time.**"
Starting with this extract, how does Stevenson present Lanyon in the novella?

You should write about:
- how Stevenson presents Lanyon in this extract
- how Stevenson presents Lanyon in the novella as a whole.

Mr Enfield & Poole

Q1   Complete the table below about these characters.

Character	Who he is	His role in the story
Enfield		
Poole		

Q2   Give two quotes which show that Enfield is concerned about reputation.

1) ....

2) ....

Q3   When he first meets Hyde, Enfield says he is returning "**from some place at the end of the world**" at 3 am. What does this suggest about Enfield?

....

....

Q4   How can you tell that Poole is loyal to Jekyll?

....

....

Q5   Poole often addresses the other characters as "**sir**". Explain what this shows about his relationships with other characters.

....

....

....

Poole's pretty tough — he dives straight into the action...

All the characters have been included for a reason — they might represent a theme or help to develop the plot. Before the exam, make sure you can write about the role of every character in the novella.

Section Two — Characters

Making Links

A great way to develop your answer is to make links between the points you've made and other parts of the text. You could write about similar events, other times characters behave in the same way or other places where a theme is presented. This page will get you thinking about how some of the main characters behave in similar ways in different parts of the novella. Try to use specific examples from the text — this will help you to develop clear links between different parts of the novella.

Q1 Read the statements below, then answer each question.

a) In 'Search for Mr Hyde', Utterson pursues Hyde to discover more about him. Find an example of another character who behaves in a similar way in 'Dr Lanyon's Narrative'.

Character: ....

Behaviour: ....

....

b) In 'Remarkable Incident of Dr Lanyon', Utterson chooses not to question Lanyon about why he has fallen out with Jekyll. Find an example of another character who behaves in a similar way in 'Incident of the Letter'.

Character: ....

Behaviour: ....

....

Q2 Fill in the table below with examples from different parts of the novella that illustrate the key point about each character. You can either use quotes or just explain what happens, as long as it's a precise example.

Character	Key Point	Example One	Example Two
Hyde			
Utterson			
Jekyll			

Practice Questions

Ahhh lovely... a page of practice questions to get stuck into. Don't worry though, these questions are designed to get you thinking about how to structure answers and improve your arguments — the more you practise, the better you'll do on the big day. So grab a brew, get comfy and start planning your answers.

Q1 Write about the ways Stevenson presents the relationship between Jekyll and Hyde. Refer to this extract and the novella as a whole.

Taken from 'Chapter Ten: Henry Jekyll's Full Statement of the Case'

When I came to myself at Lanyon's, the horror of my old friend perhaps affected me somewhat: I do not know; it was at least but a drop in the sea to the abhorrence with which I looked back upon these hours. A change had come over me. It was no longer the fear of the gallows, it was the horror of being Hyde that racked me. I received Lanyon's condemnation partly in a dream; it was partly in a dream that I came home to my own house and got into bed. I slept after the prostration of the day, with a stringent and profound slumber which not even the nightmares that wrung me could avail to break. I awoke in the morning shaken, weakened, but refreshed. I still hated and feared the thought of the brute that slept within me, and I had not of course forgotten the appalling dangers of the day before; but I was once more at home, in my own house and close to my drugs; and gratitude for my escape shone so strong in my soul that it almost rivalled the brightness of hope.
I was stepping leisurely across the court after breakfast, drinking the chill of the air with pleasure, when I was seized again with those indescribable sensations that heralded the change; and I had but the time to gain the shelter of my cabinet, before I was once again raging and freezing with the passions of Hyde. It took on this occasion a double dose to recall me to myself; and alas, six hours after, as I sat looking sadly in the fire, the pangs returned, and the drug had to be readministered.

Q2 Read from the start of 'Story of the Door' to "**might enjoy them uninterrupted.**"

a) How does Stevenson present Utterson in this extract?

b) In this chapter, Enfield discusses his initial reaction to Hyde. How does Stevenson present the characters' reactions to Hyde in the novella as a whole?
You should write about:

- how characters react when they meet Hyde
- why characters react to Hyde in this way.

Q3 Read 'Henry Jekyll's Full Statement of the Case' from "**Between these two**" to "**swallowed the transforming draught.**" Write about the characters' attitudes to temptation in this extract and in the novella as a whole.

Q4 Read 'Incident at the Window' from "**The court was very cool**" to the end of the chapter. How is Jekyll presented in this extract and in the rest of the novella?

Life in Victorian Britain

Q1 Read these statements about Victorian London.
Decide whether each one is **true** or **false**.

	True	False
London had both rich areas and slums.	☐	☐
Rich areas were often overcrowded.	☐	☐
Victorian gentlemen sometimes went to poor areas to visit pubs and brothels.	☐	☐
Smoke from factories meant that the streets were sometimes full of smog.	☐	☐

Q2 How can you tell that Hyde lives in a poor area of London?

....

....

Q3 Find an example from *Jekyll and Hyde* to back up each of the statements below.
Your examples could be events from the novella or information about characters.

a) Some Victorian gentlemen felt they had to repress their desires.

Example: ....

b) Victorian gentlemen were often secretive about activities they viewed as immoral.

Example: ....

c) Blackmail was common in the Victorian period.

Example: ....

Q4 In Victorian society, immoral behaviour was often kept
secret. How do you think Stevenson felt about this?
Use information from the text to support your answer.

....

....

....

....

© Everett Collection Inc / Alamy Stock Photo

 ☐   ☐   ☐

Reputation

Q1 Find three quotes said by Utterson which show that he cares about reputation.

Quote 1: ....

Quote 2: ....

Quote 3: ....

Q2 Read from the start of 'Henry Jekyll's Full Statement of the Case' to **"relief of sorrow and suffering."** What does this passage show about Jekyll's attitude towards reputation?

....

....

....

....

Q3 During the course of the novella, Hyde becomes more powerful than Jekyll. What do you think this suggests about Stevenson's views on the Victorian obsession with having a good reputation?

....

....

....

Q4 'Jekyll is more concerned about protecting his reputation than trying to be a moral person.' Do you agree with this statement? Explain your answer.

....

....

....

....

© Marilyn Kingwill/ArenaPAL

"Relief of sorrow and suffering" — I call them inset days...

This theme links to 'Life in Victorian Britain' on p.23 — during the 19th century, Victorian gentlemen were obsessed with their reputations and hid their immoral behaviour from respectable society.

Secrecy

Q1 Many characters keep secrets from each other. Fill in the gaps in the table below, giving one example of a secret each character keeps. Support each answer with a quote.

Character	Secret	Quote
Jekyll		
		"**What he told me in the next hour, I cannot bring my mind to set on paper.**"
	He doesn't speak to Hyde about his concerns over Jekyll's will.	

Q2 Find a quote from the text to back up each of the statements below.

a) In 'Story of the Door', Utterson and Enfield agree not to talk about Hyde again.

Quote: ....

b) Utterson wants to avoid a public scandal about Jekyll's links to Hyde.

Quote: ....

Q3 Many of the secrets in the novella are only revealed in the last two chapters. What impact does this have on the reader? Explain your answer.

....

....

....

Q4 Briefly explain how locked doors and windows are used in the novella to symbolise secrecy.

....

....

I can keep secrets, but the people I tell them to can't...

Imagine you're Jekyll. Write a paragraph explaining why you chose to keep Hyde and the potion a secret from your friends. Then, write a paragraph explaining the consequences of keeping this secret.

    Section Three — Context and Themes

Dual Nature of Man

Q1   Find a quote from the novella to back up each of the statements below.

a) Jekyll believes that everyone has a dual nature.

Quote: ....

b) Jekyll feels as if the good and bad sides of his nature are struggling against each other.

Quote: ....

c) Hyde represents the evil side of man.

Quote: ....

Q2   Using a quote from the text, explain how Jekyll might
have created a being of pure good in his experiments.

....

....

Q3   Explain whether you think evil is presented as more powerful than good in the novella.

....

....

Q4   'After he created Hyde, Jekyll became purely good.' Do you agree? Explain your answer.

....

....

....

Q5   Explain how the two doors of Jekyll's house symbolise the dual nature of man.

....

....

....

....

Section Three — Context and Themes

Q6 Fill in the table below with events that show the civilised side of man and events that show the uncivilised side of man.

Events that are civilised	Events that are uncivilised
Utterson and Enfield walk through London.	Hyde tramples over a young girl.

Q7 Find three short quotes from 'The Carew Murder Case' which show that Hyde is uncivilised.

Quote 1: ....

....

Quote 2: ....

....

Quote 3: ....

....

© Nick Collinge @ Love It Studios

Q8 Find an example of where Stevenson uses imagery to suggest that appearances can be deceiving.

....

....

Q9 Some Victorians believed that a person's appearance reflected their personality. How does Stevenson use this idea to reflect the dual nature of man in the novella?

....

....

....

....

PRACTICE TASK

I use a potion to become civilised too — it's called coffee...

On a scale from 1 to 5 (1 being completely good and 5 being completely bad), decide where you would put Jekyll and Utterson. For each character, write a couple of sentences justifying your decision.

Science and Religion

Q1 Read the paragraph below and fill in the gaps using words from the box.

In the Victorian era, most people in England were .... During this period,

.... published a book which claimed that humans were descended from

.... The theory of evolution was very .... as it went against

Christian teachings about the .... of man. People were concerned about the

idea that everyone has an uncivilised and .... side.

| Christian primitive origin Stevenson Darwin Atheist evil controversial apes |

Q2 Do you think Jekyll is religious? Explain your answer.

....

....

....

Q3 A group of Christians called Evangelicals believed that people should seek forgiveness from God by living a strict lifestyle. Think of a character from the novella who lives like this and give a quote which supports your choice.

Name of character: ....

Quote: ....

....

Q4 How does Stevenson's description of Hyde suggest that he is less evolved than Jekyll? Use a quote to support your answer.

....

....

....

....

Section Three — Context and Themes

Q5 Look at these statements about Jekyll's experiments.
Decide whether each one is **true** or **false**.

	True	False
Jekyll's experiments investigate the mystical.	☐	☐
Jekyll's experiments focus on human nature.	☐	☐
Jekyll's father told him how to make the potion.	☐	☐
The transformations cause Jekyll and Hyde agony.	☐	☐

© Nick Collinge @ Love It Studios

Q6 Briefly explain how Lanyon's scientific beliefs differ from Jekyll's.

....

....

Q7 Read 'Doctor Lanyon's Narrative' from "**Here I proceeded**" to "**no end of practical usefulness.**"
What do you think Stevenson is suggesting about science in this passage? Explain your answer.

....

....

....

Q8 After Lanyon sees Hyde's transformation, he says "**I ask myself if I believe it, and I cannot answer.**" How does Hyde's transformation challenge Lanyon's beliefs about science?

....

....

Q9 In his notebook, Jekyll writes that an earlier experiment was a "**total failure!!!**" Do you think he would class the experiment where Hyde was created as a failure? Explain your answer.

....

....

....

....

Don't have a lack of revision on your conScience...

Read 'Henry Jekyll's Full Statement of the Case' from "**I do not suppose that**" to "**hands to God.**"
Explore the importance of religion in *Jekyll and Hyde*. You should write about:
• the importance of religion in this extract
• the importance of religion in the rest of the novella.

  ☺ ☐ ☺ ☐

Section Three — Context and Themes

Writing about Context

You'll need to include relevant information about the context of the novella to get a high mark in the exam. *Jekyll and Hyde* was written in the 19th century, so you need to have an understanding of what society was like then and how attitudes to science and religion were changing. Adding contextual information and linking it to the key themes will help you to improve your answer. The questions on this page will get you thinking about context and how to use it in your responses.

Q1 Read the sample answer extracts below and underline the contextual information.

> **a)** Stevenson uses different areas of London to highlight the different personalities of Jekyll and Hyde. For example, Hyde lives in an area where "ragged children" are found in doorways. On the other hand, Jekyll lives in an area where the residents are "all doing well". In Victorian Britain, poor areas were often associated with immorality, as they were home to businesses such as brothels and gin parlours. Wealthy areas appeared more respectable. Stevenson therefore uses the contrasting images of wealth and poverty surrounding Jekyll and Hyde's houses to highlight the characters' contrasting moral natures. Hyde is surrounded by poverty and is immoral, whereas Jekyll, who is wealthy, is more moral.

> **b)** Hyde is often described as an animal. Poole claims that Hyde looks "like a monkey" and, when Hyde attacks Carew, he is described as "ape-like". Shortly before *Jekyll and Hyde* was published, Charles Darwin published a theory about the evolution of mankind, explaining that apes were ancestors of humans. The references to both 'monkeys' and 'apes' therefore suggest to the reader that Hyde is a less evolved version of Jekyll. Darwin's theory contradicted Christian teachings about the origins of mankind at the time. As a result, Stevenson's animalistic portrayal of Hyde could also suggest that Hyde is ungodly.

Q2 Write down a piece of context that could be included in the sample answer below.

> Explore how religion is presented in *Jekyll and Hyde*.

> In the novella, Stevenson often uses sinful imagery to describe the characters of Jekyll and Hyde. For example, Jekyll refers to himself as a "sinner" and Enfield compares Hyde to "Satan". These religious images are used by Stevenson to emphasise the evil that exists within both Jekyll and Hyde, as both the descriptions relate to the idea of hell.

....

....

....

....

Practice Questions

'Jekyll and Hyde' deals with a lot of different themes. It's important that you know each of the themes inside out, so here are some practice questions to help you check what you know. Try to use some background knowledge about Victorian Britain to add some context into your answers too.

Q1 Using the extract below as a starting point, write about how Stevenson presents science as horrifying in the novella.

> Taken from 'Chapter Ten: Henry Jekyll's Full Statement of the Case'
>
> I hesitated long before I put this theory to the test of practice. I knew well that I risked death; for any drug that so potently controlled and shook the very fortress of identity, might by the least scruple of an overdose or at the least in opportunity in the moment of exhibition, utterly blot out that immaterial tabernacle which I looked to it to change. But the temptation of a discovery so singular and profound, at last overcame the suggestions of alarm. I had long since prepared my tincture; I purchased at once, from a firm of wholesale chemists, a large quantity of a particular salt which I knew, from my experiments, to be the last ingredient required; and late one accursed night, I compounded the elements, watched them boil and smoke together in the glass, and when the ebullition had subsided, with a strong glow of courage, drank off the potion.
> The most racking pangs succeeded: a grinding in the bones, deadly nausea, and a horror of the spirit that cannot be exceeded at the hour of birth or death. Then these agonies began swiftly to subside, and I came to myself as if out of a great sickness. There was something strange in my sensations, something indescribably new and, from its very novelty, incredibly sweet. I felt younger, lighter, happier in body; within I was conscious of a heady recklessness, a current of disordered sensual images running like a millrace in my fancy, a solution of the bonds of obligation, an unknown but not an innocent freedom of the soul.

Q2 Read 'Remarkable Incident of Doctor Lanyon' from "**I have had a shock**" to "**respect my silence.**" Explore the importance of secrecy in this extract and in the novella as a whole. You should write about:

- how secrecy affects the events of the novella
- how secrecy affects characters' behaviour.

Q3 Read from the start of 'Henry Jekyll's Full Statement of the Case' to "**but truly two.**" How far do you agree that the novella is about the struggle between good and evil? You should refer to the extract and the novella as a whole in your answer.

Q4 Read 'Story of the Door' from "**The pair walked on**" to the end of the chapter.

a) Explain how Stevenson presents reputation in this extract.

b) Write about the importance of reputation to the characters elsewhere in the novella. You should consider:

- how important reputation is to the characters
- how this influences their behaviour.

Structure and Narrative

Q1   Why do you think Stevenson includes the story of the girl being trampled in the first chapter?

....

....

....

Q2   The reader does not find out that Jekyll and Hyde are the same person until 'Dr Lanyon's Narrative'. How does this help to create a sense of intrigue throughout the novella?

....

....

Q3   What later event does each of the following details foreshadow?   *Foreshadowing is when a writer hints about something that will happen later in the text.*

a) In 'Search for Mr Hyde', Hyde is described as having a **"murderous mixture"** of characteristics.

....

b) In 'Dr Jekyll was Quite at Ease', Jekyll is described as having **"a slyish cast"**.

....

c) In 'Incident of the Letter', Utterson says he is afraid that Hyde will murder Jekyll.

....

Q4   An embedded narrative is a story within the main narrative, e.g. Lanyon's letter to Utterson. Why do you think Stevenson uses embedded narratives in the novella?

....

....

Q5   Why do you think Stevenson does not give Hyde a first-person narrative?

....

....

Q6 Lanyon gives Utterson a letter in 'Remarkable Incident of Dr Lanyon', but the reader only learns what it says in 'Doctor Lanyon's Narrative'. Explain the impact of this.

....

....

....

Q7 Why do you think Stevenson places Lanyon's letter before Jekyll's letter?

....

....

....

Q8 In 'Dr Lanyon's Narrative', Lanyon describes the events of the novella from his own point of view. Decide whether each statement is **true** or **false**, and explain your answer.

a) There is an embedded narrative within Lanyon's letter. **True:** ☐ **False:** ☐

....

b) Lanyon reveals everything in his letter. **True:** ☐ **False:** ☐

....

c) Lanyon is honest about his emotions in the letter. **True:** ☐ **False:** ☐

....

Q9 Why do you think Stevenson uses a first-person narrative in 'Henry Jekyll's Full Statement of the Case'?

....

....

....

....

....

© Moviestore Collection/REX/Shutterstock

What 8-letter word only contains one letter? Envelope...

It's not enough to just point out the techniques Stevenson uses. In the exam, you'll need to be able to give examples of each technique you mention and then explain what effects they have on the reader.

Section Four — The Writer's Techniques

Setting and Symbolism

Q1 Read the paragraph below and fill in the gaps using the words in the box.

In the novella, Victorian London is a .... place. For example, the streets are

referred to as "**labyrinths**". This description emphasises the confusing nature of the streets as it

brings to mind .... and the feeling of being .... Stevenson

also uses darkness to make the .... seem more threatening. This is particularly

effective because darkness is linked to .... throughout the text.

| myths | crowded | mazes | language | lost | Carew | alone | setting | evil | frightening |

Q2 What makes London an effective setting for the story? Explain your answer.

....

....

Q3 Why do you think Stevenson chose to locate Hyde's
house in Soho? Use a quote to support your answer.

....

....

....

Q4 Fog is used in the novella to symbolise mystery.
Explain how Stevenson explores this symbol through:

a) fog in the streets of London

....

....

....

b) fog inside Jekyll's house

....

....

Q5 In 'The Last Night', Poole breaks down the door of Jekyll's cabinet. What does this action symbolise?

....

....

....

Q6 'In the novella, the moon symbolises imminent danger.'
Give an example from the text which shows this.

....

....

Q7 Silence is a motif in the novella — an object or idea which reappears often in a text.
Which of the following statements are true? Tick all the statements that apply.

Stevenson uses silence to create a sense of mystery throughout the novella. ☐

Lanyon is silent when he is asked about his relationship with Jekyll. ☐

London is often presented as silent and empty in the novella. ☐

Utterson and Enfield do not discuss Jekyll's strange behaviour in 'Incident at the Window'. ☐

Q8 Explain what the cane Hyde uses to kill Carew symbolises in the novella.

....

....

....

....

Q9 What do you think Jekyll's mirror symbolises? Explain your answer.

....

....

....

Fog in the house? Time to get the central heating fixed...

Stevenson often uses symbols more than once to make a point about characters and themes. When you're thinking about a symbol, it's worth thinking about whether it crops up anywhere else in the text.

 ☐ ☐ ☐   **Section Four — The Writer's Techniques**

Language and Dialogue

Q1 Read the paragraph below and fill in the gaps using the words in the box.

In 'Story of the Door', Enfield uses extremely .... language,

describing Hyde as "**like a damned Juggernaut**" when he trampled the child.

This .... is used to emphasise Hyde's overwhelming power

and .... In his account of Carew's murder, Stevenson

explains that Carew's "**bones were audibly shattered**". This sensory description

creates a sense of .... for the reader.

simple
relief
metaphor
simile
vivid
horror
aggression
personality
humour
godliness

Q2 In 'Search for Mr Hyde', Utterson says "**If he be Mr Hyde... I shall be Mr Seek.**"
How does this quote differ from Utterson's language elsewhere? Explain your answer.

....

....

....

Q3 Find short quotes to back up the following statements about Jekyll's language.

a) In 'Dr Jekyll was Quite at Ease', Jekyll's language is abrupt.

Quote: ....

b) In 'Incident of the Letter', Jekyll's language is misleading.

Quote: ....

c) In 'The Last Night', Jekyll's language in his letter to Utterson is sorrowful.

Quote: ....

Q4 Briefly explain how Lanyon's language changes between 'Search for Mr Hyde'
and 'Remarkable Incident of Dr Lanyon'. Use a quote to support your answer.

....

....

....

....

Section Four — The Writer's Techniques

Q5 Read 'Incident at the Window' from "**The court was very cool**" to "**with a smile.**" What does the language in this passage suggest about Jekyll's state of mind? Explain your answer.

© Marilyn Kingwill/ArenaPAL

....

....

....

....

Q6 Find a quote from Poole that shows he speaks differently to the other characters. In your own words, explain what this shows about Poole.

Quote: ....

....

Explanation: ....

....

Q7 Read 'Search for Mr Hyde' from "**Mr Hyde shrank back**" to "**that is not fitting language.**" How does Hyde's language in this passage reflect his character?

....

....

....

Q8 When Utterson hears something shocking, he sometimes says "**Tut-tut**". What does this tell you about his character? Explain your answer.

....

....

Q9 The language in the main narrative is formal and matter-of-fact. How does this make the events of the novella more shocking?

....

....

....

Section Four — The Writer's Techniques

Q10 Read 'The Carew Murder Case', then find an example of each of the language techniques below. Explain the effect of each example.

Technique	Example	Effect
Metaphor	"a great flame of anger"	
Metaphor		
Personification	"mournful reinvasion of darkness"	
Personification		

Q11 Stevenson often gives detailed descriptions of events in the novella. Give an example of an event that is described in detail, and explain the effect of this description.

Example: ....

Explanation: ....

Q12 Stevenson often uses similes to describe Hyde's appearance. Why do you think he does this?

....

....

Q13 Read 'Henry Jekyll's Full Statement of the Case'. Find one example of where Stevenson uses language to create sympathy for Jekyll and explain its effect.

....

....

....

Similes make Stevenson's writing as vivid as a picture...

Read 'Remarkable Incident of Dr Lanyon' from "**A week afterwards**" to "**its inscrutable recluse.**" **How does Stevenson present Utterson as moral in *Jekyll and Hyde*?** You should consider:

- how Stevenson presents Utterson as moral in this extract
- how Stevenson presents Utterson as moral in the novella as a whole.

'Jekyll and Hyde' as a Gothic Novel

Q1 *Jekyll and Hyde* has many features of a Gothic novel.
Fill in the table with examples of these features.

Gothic Feature	Example in *Jekyll and Hyde*
There is often a character who is an 'outsider' in society.	
Science is often presented as unsettling.	
There is often an evil villain.	
The settings are usually mysterious.	

Q2 For each of the following statements, explain how
Jekyll and Hyde differs from typical Gothic novels.

a) Gothic novels are usually set in abandoned castles or faraway places.

....

b) Gothic villains are often beautiful.

....

c) Gothic novels often include a female character who needs saving from something or someone.

....

Q3 Based on your answers to Q1 and Q2, do you think *Jekyll and Hyde*
should be seen as a traditional Gothic novel? Explain your answer.

....

....

....

....

Gothic literature — it's not all eyeliner and skinny jeans...

Gothic novels are often set in faraway places. Write a paragraph explaining why you think Stevenson
set the novella in the streets of London, and the impact this could have had on Victorian readers.

Working with Extracts

In the exam, you'll be given an extract from the book to analyse. The examiner is expecting you to write about the extract in detail, so it's important that you think about it carefully before you begin to write your answer. This page will help you to develop the main skills that you'll need. When you're writing about the extract, the P.E.E.D. method is your faithful friend — see page 14 for more.

Taken from 'Chapter Four: The Carew Murder Case'

And then all of a sudden he broke out in a great flame of anger, stamping with his foot, brandishing the cane, and carrying on (as the maid described it) like a madman. The old gentleman took a step back, with the air of one very much surprised and a trifle hurt; and at that Mr Hyde broke out of all bounds and clubbed him to the earth. And next moment, with ape-like fury, he was trampling his victim under foot, and hailing down a storm of blows, under which the bones were audibly shattered and the body jumped upon the roadway. At the horror of these sights and sounds, the maid fainted.

It was two o'clock when she came to herself and called for the police. The murderer was gone long ago; but there lay his victim in the middle of the lane, incredibly mangled. The stick with which the deed had been done, although it was of some rare and very tough and heavy wood, had broken in the middle under the stress of this insensate cruelty; and one splintered half had rolled in the neighbouring gutter — the other, without doubt, had been carried away by the murderer. A purse and gold watch were found upon the victim; but no cards or papers, except a sealed and stamped envelope, which he had been probably carrying to the post, and which bore the name and address of Mr. Utterson.

Q1 Read through the extract above and describe where in the story it comes from. Think about what has just happened and what is about to happen.

....

....

....

Q2 In the extract, the Narrator states that Hyde attacks his victim with **"ape-like fury"**. Explain what this quote suggests about Hyde's temper.

....

....

Q3 Pick out a word or phrase from the extract which suggests that Hyde's attack on Carew is brutal, then explain how it does this.

....

....

Q4 In this extract, Hyde behaves violently. Write down an example of when Hyde is violent elsewhere in the novella.

....

Practice Questions

Now that you've got yourself up to speed with the writer's techniques, it's time to have a go at these practice questions. Make sure you know what the question is asking you to do, and then set aside some time to do a rough plan before you start on your answer — otherwise you might end up in a bit of a pickle.

Q1 Using the extract below as a starting point, explain how Stevenson creates a mysterious atmosphere in the novella.

> <u>Taken from 'Chapter Nine: The Last Night'</u>
>
> It was a wild, cold, seasonable night of March, with a pale moon, lying on her back as though the wind had tilted her, and a flying wrack of the most diaphanous and lawny texture. The wind made talking difficult, and flecked the blood into the face. It seemed to have swept the streets unusually bare of passengers, besides; for Mr Utterson thought he had never seen that part of London so deserted. He could have wished it otherwise; never in his life had he been conscious of so sharp a wish to see and touch his fellow-creatures; for struggle as he might, there was borne in upon his mind a crushing anticipation of calamity. The square, when they got there, was all full of wind and dust, and the thin trees in the garden were lashing themselves along the railing. Poole, who had kept all the way a pace or two ahead, now pulled up in the middle of the pavement, and in spite of the biting weather, took off his hat and mopped his brow with a red pocket-handkerchief. But for all the hurry of his coming, these were not the dews of exertion that he wiped away, but the moisture of some strangling anguish; for his face was white and his voice, when he spoke, harsh and broken.
> "Well, sir," he said, "here we are, and God grant there be nothing wrong."
> "Amen, Poole," said the lawyer.
> Thereupon the servant knocked in a very guarded manner; the door was opened on the chain; and a voice asked from within, "Is that you, Poole?"

Q2 Read 'Doctor Lanyon's Narrative' from "**It is well**" to the end of the chapter. How is science presented as unnatural by Stevenson in this extract and in the novella as a whole?

Q3 Read from the start of 'Incident of the Letter' to "**in a changed voice.**" Explore the significance of setting in this extract and in the novella as a whole.

Q4 Read 'The Last Night' from "**Well, sir,**" to "**red baize of the cabinet door.**"

a) Explain how Stevenson creates suspense in this extract. Use quotes to back up your ideas.

b) In this extract, Poole tells Utterson that he fears for Jekyll's well-being. How is fear presented by Stevenson elsewhere in the novella? You should write about:
   • how different characters' fears are presented
   • how characters are affected by fear.

Understanding the Question

Underline key words in the question

Q1 Underline the key words in the following questions. The first one has been done for you.

a) <u>To what extent</u> does Stevenson <u>present</u> <u>Hyde</u> as an <u>evil</u> <u>character</u>?

b) Explain how the theme of religion is presented in *Jekyll and Hyde*.

c) Write about how the relationship between Jekyll and Hyde changes throughout the novella.

d) How is the theme of reputation presented in *Jekyll and Hyde*?

e) Explore the importance of secrecy in *Jekyll and Hyde*.

f) Write about the importance of Utterson in *Jekyll and Hyde*.

g) How does Stevenson create a fearful atmosphere in the novella?

Make sure you understand exam language

Q2 Match each exam question to the correct explanation of what you would need to do to answer it. You'll only need to use each white box once.

a) To what extent does Stevenson present Hyde as an evil character?	**1)** Analyse how a character contributes to the novella's plot and message.
b) Explore the importance of secrecy in *Jekyll and Hyde*.	**2)** Analyse the techniques Stevenson uses to produce a certain effect.
c) How does Stevenson create a fearful atmosphere in the novella?	**3)** Analyse how far a description of a character is correct.
d) Write about the importance of Utterson in *Jekyll and Hyde*.	**4)** Analyse how a theme contributes to the novella's plot and message.
e) Explain how the theme of religion is presented in *Jekyll and Hyde*.	**5)** Analyse the way Stevenson writes about a theme in the novella.

Exams can be scary, but don't just run and Hyde...

Understanding what the question is asking you to do is the first step towards writing a great answer. That's why it's important to take your time in the exam, read the question carefully and make sure you're on the right track.

Making a Rough Plan

Jot down your main ideas

Q1 Look at the exam question below, then complete the spider diagram with at least three more main points for answering it.

Don't forget to underline the key words in the question before you start.

Stevenson shows that Hyde's attack on Carew was vicious.

Read 'Henry Jekyll's Full Statement of the Case' from "**Instantly the spirit of hell**" to "**ground the key under my heel!**" Explain how Stevenson presents Hyde as violent in this extract and in the novella as a whole.

Put your main points and examples in a logical order

Q2 Choose your three main points from Q1 and fill in the plan below, adding evidence (a quote or an example from the text) for each point.

(Introduction)

Point One: ....

Evidence: ....

Point Two: ....

Evidence: ....

Point Three: ....

Evidence: ....

(Conclusion)

Make a plan and you'll Carewse through the exam...

It's a good idea to spend five minutes or so on a rough plan before you start writing — keep referring back to it while you're writing your spectacularly brilliant essay so you don't lose your thread and go off on a tangent.

Making Links

Make links with other parts of the text

Q1 Look at the exam question and the table below. Complete the table with other relevant parts of the text which could be used to back up each point.

> Explore how the theme of reputation is presented in the novella as a whole.

Point	Example 1	Example 2
Maintaining a good reputation is important.	Jekyll tells Utterson that he cares more for his "own character" than for Hyde.	
A person's reputation can often disguise their real nature.	Jekyll has a sinful side, but still has a good reputation.	
The gentlemen are reluctant to spread rumours about others.	In the first chapter, Enfield doesn't disclose Jekyll's name to Utterson.	

Extend your essay with other examples

You won't have time to do really detailed planning in the exam, so you should get into the habit of quickly thinking of links when you're doing practice questions.

Q2 Look back at the points you included in your plan in Q2 on p.43. For each point, write down another example from a different part of the text that you could include in your essay.

Example for Point One: ....

....

Example for Point Two: ....

....

Example for Point Three: ....

....

Time to unleash your inner detective — start making links...

Making links helps you to compare and contrast how themes and characters are presented at different points in the novella. It also helps you to show the examiner that you know the text inside out and back to front.

Structuring Your Answer

P.E.E.D. stands for Point, Example, Explain, Develop

Q1 Read the following extract from an exam answer. Label each aspect of P.E.E.D.

> Lanyon disapproves of the nature of Jekyll's scientific experiments. This is implied when Jekyll claims that Lanyon called his work "scientific heresies". 'Heresy' can mean a belief or action that goes against the teachings of God, which might suggest that Lanyon considers Jekyll's experiments to be ungodly. Most Victorians were religious and believed that humans were created by God. As such, it is likely that Victorian readers would have shared Lanyon's belief that Jekyll's experiments were indecent.

Embedding quotes is a great way to give evidence

Q2 Rewrite the following sentences so that a short part of the quote is embedded in each one.

a) Lanyon believes that Jekyll has gone mad — "He began to go wrong, wrong in mind".

....

b) Jekyll was scared of Hyde — "I still hated and feared the thought of the brute that slept within".

....

Structure your answer using the P.E.E.D. method

Q3 Use the P.E.E.D. method to structure a paragraph on your first point from Q2 on page 43.

Point: ....

....

Example: ....

....

Explain: ....

....

Develop: ....

....

Use P.E.E.D. and you'll be flushed with success...

Using the P.E.E.D. method might take a little bit of getting used to, but it's definitely worth the effort. It'll help you to structure your paragraphs well and best of all, it'll encourage you to write well-developed answers.

Introductions and Conclusions

Give a clear answer to the question in your introduction

Q1 Read the introductions below, then decide which is better. Explain your choice.

> How does Stevenson create a fearful atmosphere in the novella?

a)

> At times, *Jekyll and Hyde* has a very fearful atmosphere. Stevenson sets a lot of events at night, which creates fear because it makes the novella seem eerie. For example, Hyde's murder of Carew happens at night. This also links darkness with Hyde's character. The fact that Hyde is associated with darkness makes him seem even more intriguing to the reader.

b)

> Stevenson uses several techniques to create a fearful atmosphere in the novella. His use of settings evokes fear, particularly the way he presents the streets of London as threatening. In addition, the way darkness frequently features in the story creates a fearful atmosphere, as it increases the sense of mystery and tension for the reader.

Better intro: .... Reason: ....

....

....

....

Don't write any new points in your conclusion

Q2 Read this conclusion to the exam question in Q1, then explain how it could be improved.

> In conclusion, creating a fearful atmosphere is important to *Jekyll and Hyde*. The fearful atmosphere keeps the reader interested by increasing the tension. The unnatural and unpredictable nature of Hyde's character adds to this fear, as does Stevenson's suggestion that we all have the potential for evil.

....

....

....

....

....

I love writing conclusions — it's such a funny looking word...

Test your skills by writing an introduction and a conclusion for the exam question on p.43. Think about the good and bad examples on this page and use the points from your spider diagram to form your main ideas.

Writing about Context

Make sure you can link the novella to its context

Q1   Match each statement with the relevant contextual information.

a) Stevenson often refers to Hyde using animalistic terms.	**1)** In Victorian society, people were supposed to appear respectable by not giving into their immoral desires.
b) Jekyll tries to ignore his temptations to become Hyde after the murder of Carew.	**2)** In the 19th century, biologist Charles Darwin published a theory that humans had evolved from apes.
c) Jekyll thinks that all humans have a moral side and an immoral side.	**3)** In Victorian Britain, many Christians believed that humans were naturally sinful.

Include context in your answer

Q2   Read the sample answer below, underlining the contextual information.

> The dual nature of man is used to highlight the hypocrisy that existed in the Victorian upper class. Jekyll wears the "thick cloak" of Hyde to conceal his immoral, less respectable side. This suggests that he feels the need to hide his true nature from society by presenting a more morally acceptable version of himself to others. His behaviour reflects the pressures that many gentlemen were under in 19th-century society to maintain an air of respectability. These pressures are at the heart of Jekyll's conflicted nature, as even before he created Hyde he claims that he was bound to a "duplicity of life".

Q3   Write a paragraph using your second point from page 43.
Include contextual information and use the P.E.E.D. method.

....

....

....

....

....

....

Don't take the text out of context — otherwise con'll be lonely...

You'll have to include some context if you want a good mark in your exam. Think about how traditional Victorian values and beliefs might have shaped Stevenson's ideas and how he conveys these ideas in *Jekyll and Hyde*.

Linking Ideas and Paragraphs

Link your ideas so your argument is easy to follow

Q1   Rewrite the sample answer below so that the ideas are clearly linked.

> The characters of Utterson and Enfield both ignore unpleasant realities. Enfield talks about the trampled young girl in a matter-of-fact tone. Utterson chooses not to read Lanyon's letter. They refuse to engage with anything scandalous or dishonourable. Secrecy has an important role in the novella.

....

....

....

....

....

Q2   Write a paragraph using your third point from p.43. Make sure your ideas are properly linked.

....

....

....

....

....

Show how your paragraphs follow on from each other

Q3   Look at the three paragraphs you have written on pages 45, 47 and in Q2 on this page. Write down linking words or phrases you could use to link them together in your answer.

Paragraphs to link	Linking word or phrase
p.45 and p.47	
p.47 and p.48	

Linking phrases are like sat nav directions, only less annoying...

Linking phrases are great, but only if your ideas are in a logical order to begin with. That's why it's useful to make a plan — it doesn't have to be really detailed, but it's good to know where you're going before you start.

Marking Answer Extracts

Get familiar with the mark scheme

Grade band	An answer at this level...
8-9	• shows an insightful and critical personal response to the text • closely and perceptively analyses how the writer uses language, form and structure to create meaning and affect the reader, making use of highly relevant subject terminology • supports arguments with well-integrated, highly relevant and precise examples from the text • gives a detailed exploration of the relationship between the text and its context • uses highly varied vocabulary and sentence types, with mostly accurate spelling and punctuation
6-7	• shows a critical and observant personal response to the text • includes a thorough exploration of how the writer uses language, form and structure to create meaning and affect the reader, making use of appropriate subject terminology • supports arguments with integrated, well-chosen examples from the text • explores the relationship between the text and its context • uses a substantial range of vocabulary and sentence types, with generally accurate spelling and punctuation
4-5	• shows a thoughtful and clear personal response to the text • examines how the writer uses language, form and structure to create meaning and affect the reader, making some use of relevant subject terminology • integrates appropriate examples from the text • shows an understanding of contextual factors • uses a moderate range of vocabulary and sentence types, without spelling and punctuation errors which make the meaning unclear

Have a go at marking an answer extract

Q1   Using the mark scheme, put the sample answer extract below in a grade band and explain why.

> How does Stevenson present Utterson's relationships with other characters in the novella?

> Stevenson presents the relationship between Utterson and Enfield as unusual because they apear to have nothing in common with each other. For example, the reader is told that "It was a nut to crack for many, what these two could see in each other". This suggests that the relationship of these two Victorian gentlemen puzzles others, and introduces the idea that two people can be very diferent but still be connected. This important theme is explored later by the relationship between Jekyll and Hyde.

Grade band: ....   Reason: ....

....

....

....

Marking Answer Extracts

Have a look at these extracts from answers to the question on p.49

Q1 For each extract, say what grade band you think it is in, then underline an example of where it meets each of the mark scheme criteria. Label each underlined point to show what it achieves.

---

a) Utterson is presented as someone who forms close friendships gradually, but remains extremely loyal to the people he becomes attached to. For example, his feelings for his friends are compared to "ivy"; this description creates a vivid image of Utterson's emotions as slow-growing but tenacious, implying that once he has a bond with someone, he will remain firmly attached to them indefinitely. However, the comparison to ivy could also be viewed in a negative way: ivy is toxic and difficult to get rid of. This could hint that Utterson's attachment to other people is sometimes stifling and unwelcome, which is supported later in the novella when Jekyll responds "sharply" to Utterson's advice about his will.

Nonetheless, many of Utterson's relationships are portrayed as genuinely warm and affectionate. When Utterson first visits Lanyon, the narrator says that Lanyon "sprang up from his chair" to welcome Utterson; the verb "sprang" creates a sense of how quickly Lanyon moves, which emphasises how pleased he is to see Utterson and suggests that he is very fond of him. It also makes Lanyon seem very energetic and outgoing, which creates a contrast with Utterson, who is presented as more subdued and reserved. Utterson's subdued nature reflects the way that many Victorian gentlemen felt it necessary to repress their emotions to maintain a good reputation. Therefore, by showing Utterson to be reserved, Stevenson presents him as a character whose relationships are governed by the strict conventions of Victorian society, rather than one who is uncaring or emotionless.

Grade band: ....

---

b) Throughout the novella, Utterson repeatedly demonstrates his loyalty to Jekyll, which reveals how close a relationship they have. For example, after Carew's murder, Utterson leads the police to the home of Hyde, who he knows to be "Henry Jekyll's favourite", but does not tell them about Hyde's link to Jekyll. Stevenson uses the word "favourite" to show that Utterson knows how close Jekyll and Hyde are, but withholds this information from the police. This suggests that he would protect his friends' reputations even if they had committed a crime. This implies that Utterson values friendship above doing what is morally right, which shows how important friendship is to him. However, his concern for Jekyll's reputation also highlights the hypocrisy in Victorian society, where people were more concerned with appearing respectable than actually doing the right thing.

Utterson and Jekyll's relationship deteriorates through the course of the novella, and Stevenson uses the structure of the text to demonstrate this. In 'Dr Jekyll was Quite at Ease', Jekyll tells Utterson that he would trust him "before any man alive". The idea that he trusts Utterson above all over men in the world emphasises the strength of their trust and implies that Utterson is his closest friend. Later in the novella, in 'Remarkable Incident of Doctor Lanyon', Jekyll repeatedly refuses to admit Utterson into his house. This suggests that Jekyll's confidence in Utterson isn't as strong as he claimed, as he cannot trust him with his secret. This could hint that Utterson's relationships with his other friends are also not as close as they first appear; this is supported by the fact that Lanyon does not immediately confide in Utterson after learning Jekyll's secret.

Grade band: ....

Marking a Whole Answer

Q1 Read the sample answer below. On page 52, put it in a grade band and explain your decision.

Read 'Henry Jekyll's Full Statement of the Case' from "**I must here speak**" to "**the face of Henry Jekyll.**" Explain how the dual nature of man is presented in this extract and in the novella as a whole.

If it helps you, label examples of where the answer meets the mark scheme criteria.

In *Jekyll and Hyde*, Stevenson presents the dual nature of man as a division between good and evil. Stevenson explores this division through his presentation of Jekyll and Hyde. Jekyll struggles with his dual nature and views it as something to be overcome, but his attempts to do so result in the creation of an evil being. The conflict between the two sides of human nature is also reflected in other characters, and in the setting of the novella. By making the dual aspects of man's nature such a fundamental part of the text, and by showing the disastrous consequences of trying to divide them, Stevenson suggests that the two sides cannot be separated from one another.

Stevenson uses the characters of Jekyll and Hyde to demonstrate the dual nature of man. This is made clear in the extract, when Jekyll describes his first sight of Hyde and the realisation that he is "pure evil", in contrast to Jekyll's own "divided countenance". This demonstrates that Jekyll has succeeded in separating and giving form to the evil side of his own nature, while he remains a mixture of both good and evil. Throughout the novella, Hyde is described in Satanic terms, for example Utterson says he has "Satan's signature" on his face and Jekyll calls him a "child of Hell". As Victorian society was very religious, this imagery would have made Hyde seem more frightening, emphasising Stevenson's message about the dangers of trying to challenge the duality of human nature.

The extract explores Jekyll's realisation that it is not only himself who is composed of two conflicting sides, but that "all human beings" are "commingled out of good and evil". The word "commingled" creates the impression that the two sides are so closely linked that they cannot be truly separated. Jekyll describes this duality as "the curse of mankind", suggesting that he views it as a great misfortune that has been inflicted on humans. The word "curse" links Jekyll's views to the supernatural, hinting that he believes that by 'breaking' the curse of man's dual nature, he can free mankind from suffering. However, by attempting to change human nature, Jekyll is playing God; the fact that this results in his death could be seen as a punishment for his blasphemy.

In addition, Stevenson uses the structure and narrative voice of Jekyll's embedded narrative in the final chapter to show how his identity is divided. At the start of the chapter, Stevenson uses Jekyll as a first-person narrator. However, in the extract, Jekyll begins to refer to himself in the third person as "Henry Jekyll". This shift in Jekyll's narrative voice makes his identity seem unstable; it is as if he is no longer in control of who he is. Stevenson may be implying that the boundary between Jekyll and Hyde is breaking down. The way that Jekyll's use of the third person to talk about himself becomes more frequent as the chapter progresses emphasises how much his original identity has been weakened by his attempts to overcome his dual nature.

Jekyll's appearance also reflects the dual nature of man: he has "every mark of capacity and kindness", but he also has a "blackness" around his eyes, reflecting the inner evil that he is hiding, as well as a "something of a slyish cast". Here, the repeated 's' sounds create sibilance; this emphasises a sinister side to Jekyll that hints at the duplicity of his nature. These physical features indicate that Jekyll has lived with the two sides of his nature for so long that they have left tangible marks upon him. This further emphasises how intertwined the two aspects of human nature are, and how impossible they are to separate.

This answer continues on p.52.

Marking a Whole Answer

Stevenson uses setting to symbolise the division in Jekyll's identity, which further emphasises his views on the duality of human nature. This is demonstrated by Jekyll's house, the front door of which "wore a great air of wealth and comfort", while the laboratory door "was blistered and distained", an image that suggests damage and corruption. Therefore, the front door represents Jekyll and the good in man, while the back door represents Hyde and man's evil. However, the two doors are part of the same building, and therefore highlight Stevenson's belief that the two sides of human nature are part of a whole, and cannot be separated.

The dual nature of man is also explored through Stevenson's use of elements of the Gothic form; he uses the Gothic convention of the 'double' to emphasise the duality of Jekyll's nature. For example, Jekyll's narrative reveals his belief that "man is not truly one, but truly two." This shows that Jekyll views the two sides of his character as entirely separate, and believes that everyone is made up of two such conflicting personalities. However, unlike most Gothic novels where the 'double' is two separate people, Stevenson instead presents the 'double' as two sides of the same person. By doing this, Stevenson emphasises his message to the reader that we all have evil within us.

Throughout the novella, Stevenson links the idea of a split between good and evil with a split between people's public and private lives. On the surface, the characters are virtuous, for example Jekyll "had always been known for charities". However, there are hints that in private they all indulge in behaviour that they would view as sinful. For example, Enfield mentions coming home at "about three o'clock" in the morning, but does not reveal what he was doing. This divide between public and private life links to ideas of Victorian morality: gentlemen were expected to avoid 'sinful' activities such as drinking and sex, leading many to practise them in secret. Stevenson uses the theme of duality to comment on the hypocrisy of the society in which he lived, where there was such a contrast between public appearance and private behaviour.

Overall, Stevenson uses a variety of techniques to present the dual nature of man. This duality is presented most distinctly in the characters of Jekyll and Hyde, but also through the other characters and the settings of the novella. Jekyll's attempts to separate the two sides of his nature ultimately fail, and lead to the deaths of both Jekyll and Hyde. This suggests that Stevenson believed that the two sides of man's nature were not intended to be separate and that humans should recognise and accept their own dual nature.

Grade band: .... Reasons: ....

....

....

....

....

....

....

Grade bands: when rock and indie just don't cut it...

It's no good ignoring mark schemes and grade bands — you should keep them in mind when you're writing your essays. That way, you'll get really familiar with what you need to do to get a good mark in the exam.

Writing Well

The examiners are ready and waiting to award you marks for writing well — so don't let the opportunity pass you by. Including a variety of vocabulary, relevant technical terms and different sentence structures will improve the quality of your writing. At the end of the exam, read through your work to check that you haven't made any spelling, punctuation and grammar (SPaG) mistakes. If you spot any, just cross them out and write your corrections neatly above. It's as simple as that.

Q1 Read the sample answer below. Underline the SPaG mistakes, then correct them. One has been done for you.

> Jekyll
> As the novella progresses, <u>Jeckyll</u> gradually realises that he can no longer control the
>
> "brute" inside him. This is shown when Jekyll transforms into Hyde without drinkin
>
> the potion. Instead of allowing hyde to control him, Jekyll locks himself in his cabinet
>
> and dyes. His death is tragic; which causes the reader to sympathise with him.

Q2 Rewrite the following sentences, using appropriate language for the exam.

   a) Jekyll tries to hide his bad side so he looks good in front of his friends.

   ....

   ....

   b) Stevenson makes London seem like a scary place where dangerous things happen.

   ....

   ....

   c) Lanyon's speech starts off happy but becomes more serious later on.

   ....

   ....

   d) Carew is a nice person who lots of people seem to look up to.

   ....

   ....

Practice Questions

Now it's time to use what you've learned in this section to have a go at these practice questions. For each one, spend about five minutes doing a rough plan and give yourself about 40 minutes to write your answer. Leave some time for checking at the end — and remember that you don't have to do them all at once.

Q1 Using the extract below as a starting point, explain how Stevenson creates excitement in *Jekyll and Hyde*.

> <u>Taken from 'Chapter Eight: The Last Night'</u>
>
> "Jekyll," cried Utterson, with a loud voice, "I demand to see you." He paused a moment, but there came no reply. "I give you fair warning, our suspicions are aroused, and I must and shall see you," he resumed; "if not by fair means, then by foul — if not of your consent, then by brute force!"
>
> "Utterson," said the voice, "for God's sake, have mercy!"
>
> "Ah, that's not Jekyll's voice — it's Hyde's!" cried Utterson. "Down with the door, Poole." Poole swung the axe over his shoulder; the blow shook the building, and the red baize door leaped against the lock and hinges. A dismal screech, as of mere animal terror, rang from the cabinet. Up went the axe again, and again the panels crashed and the frame bounded; four times the blow fell; but the wood was tough and the fittings were of excellent workmanship; and it was not until the fifth, that the lock burst in sunder and the wreck of the door fell inwards on the carpet.
>
> The besiegers, appalled by their own riot and the stillness that had succeeded, stood back a little and peered in. There lay the cabinet before their eyes in the quiet lamplight, a good fire glowing and chattering on the hearth, the kettle singing its thin strain, a drawer or two open, papers neatly set forth on the business table, and nearer the fire, the things laid out for tea: the quietest room, you would have said, and, but for the glazed presses full of chemicals, the most commonplace that night in London.

Q2 Read 'Henry Jekyll's Full Statement of the Case' from "**It is useless**" to "**to release himself at the last moment?**"

  a) In this extract, how does Stevenson use the character of Jekyll to demonstrate the dangers of science?

  b) Explore the importance of science in the rest of the novella.

Q3 Read 'Incident of the Letter' from "**'And now,' said Mr Utterson**" to "**his past suspicions.**" How is Jekyll presented as a victim by Stevenson in this extract and the novella as a whole?

Q4 Read 'Henry Jekyll's Full Statement of the Case' from "**I was stepping leisurely**" to "**the offices of life.**" How does Stevenson use language to create a sense of horror in the extract and in the novella as a whole?

Answers

Section One — Analysis of Chapters

Page 2: Story of the Door
Mr Utterson learns about Hyde from Mr Enfield

1. E.g. Utterson seems to be a typical Victorian gentleman. He is described as "austere" and "dreary". He is also described as "lovable", which suggests he is liked by others.
2. E.g. I do agree because although they go for regular walks together, they don't usually talk to each other. **Or** e.g. I do not agree because both are presented as typical Victorian gentlemen, and both are "ashamed" of talking about other people.
3. a) True: "a little man"
   b) False: "some damned Juggernaut."
   c) True: "I had taken a loathing to my gentleman"
4. E.g. This suggests that they understand the importance of reputation and don't want to associate Jekyll's name with anything immoral.

Page 3: Search for Mr Hyde
Mr Utterson reads Jekyll's will

1. The statements should be numbered 2, 3, 1, 5, 4.
2. E.g. Because Jekyll is leaving his entire fortune to Hyde.
3. a) He is sociable and friendly: "he sprang up from his chair and welcomed him"
   b) Hyde instinctively tries to hide from Utterson: "Mr Hyde shrank back with a hissing intake of the breath."
   c) He suspects that Hyde might kill Jekyll: "he may grow impatient to inherit."
4. E.g. It has "a great air of wealth and comfort", but because it is "plunged in darkness" it also seems slightly sinister.

Page 4: Dr Jekyll was Quite at Ease
Utterson confronts Jekyll about his friendship with Hyde

1. He thinks Jekyll's experiments go against religious teachings.
2. E.g. It suggests that Jekyll's evil side may be close to the surface, as even the mention of Hyde starts to bring out hints of it.
3. E.g. Jekyll is cautious with his use of language, and he refuses to answer Utterson's questions about Hyde.
4. Hyde, Victorian, reputations, contrast, character (other answers are also possible)
5. Utterson promises to honour Jekyll's will if he dies or disappears.

Task:
Here are some points you might have included about Jekyll:
- In 'Story of the Door', Jekyll is known to be associated with Mr Hyde, but nobody knows how. This makes Jekyll seem mysterious.
- Jekyll is shown to be friendly. In 'Dr Jekyll was Quite at Ease', Jekyll has a "warm affection" for Utterson and speaks fondly of him, calling him "My good Utterson".
- Jekyll is secretive. He won't disclose his affairs to Utterson, telling him it is a "private matter". This is particularly secretive because Utterson is Jekyll's friend and has been shown to be trustworthy.

Here are some points you might have included about Hyde:
- He's disturbing. The reader meets him for the first time in 'Search for Mr Hyde', when the Narrator says Hyde "snarled aloud". This suggests he is wild and inhuman.
- He seems immoral. In the account told by Enfield to Utterson in 'Story of the Door', Hyde "trampled calmly" over a child. He doesn't seem to have a conscience and is forced to pay compensation.
- He seems secretive. He is initially hesitant to show Utterson his face and disappears with "extraordinary quickness" into the house.

Here are some points you might have included about Enfield:
- He is discreet. In 'Story of the Door', he says he has "a rule" not to ask too many questions if they are likely to have large consequences.
- He seems respectful. He refuses to gossip about Jekyll.
- He has a less respectable side. He sees Hyde trampling a girl when out at 3am. The reader is left to wonder what he was doing out at that time of night.

Page 5: The Carew Murder Case
Hyde murders Danvers Carew

1. E.g. Carew is described as "innocent" and he speaks to Hyde in a "very pretty manner of politeness." This suggests that he hasn't done anything to cause the attack.
2. E.g. Stevenson wants to demonstrate Hyde's barbarity to the reader and create a sense of horror.
3. E.g. "trampled calmly over the child's body" / "broke out in a great flame of anger".
4. a) False: "a dingy street"
   b) True: "furnished with luxury and good taste."
   c) True: "the other half of the stick was found"

Page 6: Incident of the Letter
Jekyll claims that Hyde has left forever

1. Stevenson creates a mysterious atmosphere. The laboratory is eerily "silent" and is covered in "fog".
2. a) He wanted to inherit Jekyll's fortune: "it was Hyde who dictated the terms in your will"
   b) He is worried it will damage Jekyll's reputation: "If it came to a trial, your name might appear.'"
   c) He wants Utterson to believe that Hyde has gone: "I bind my honour to you that I am done with him"
3. Utterson is relieved because Jekyll is prioritising his own reputation over Hyde.
4. Jekyll has forged the note for Hyde.

Page 7: Remarkable Incident of Dr Lanyon
Lanyon dies after a terrible shock

1. true, true, false
2. E.g. "his days are counted" / "Lanyon declared himself a doomed man."
3. E.g. Stevenson mentions Jekyll's "death or disappearance" — this was also mentioned in Jekyll's will in 'Search for Mr Hyde'. This second reference increases Utterson's concern because he can't explain why Jekyll might expect to die or disappear.
4. E.g. This suggests that Utterson is a trustworthy character. Despite his curiosity, he respects Lanyon and follows his instructions.
5. E.g. Lanyon's death was very mysterious but seems to be linked to Jekyll, so Utterson is afraid.

Task: Here are some points you might have included:
- 'Search for Mr Hyde': "hearty, healthy, dapper, red-faced gentleman" / "boisterous and decided manner" / "shock of hair prematurely white"
- 'Remarkable Incident of Dr Lanyon': "The rosy man had grown pale" / "his flesh had fallen away" / "visibly balder and older"

Page 8: Incident at the Window
Jekyll locks himself away

1. This short chapter increases the pace of the plot, which keeps the reader in suspense and increases tension.
2. transformations, terror, secret, confused, intrigued (other answers are also possible)
3. E.g. Jekyll's expression of "abject terror" in this chapter suggests he is nervous and fearful, whereas in 'Dr Jekyll was Quite at Ease', he was able to control his emotions.

56

Answers

4. E.g. They are both silent for a long time after seeing Jekyll. When they do try to talk, they are both "pale" and have "an answering horror in their eyes." Utterson can only say "God forgive us".
5. E.g. "froze the very blood of the two gentlemen below."

Page 9: The Last Night
Utterson finds Hyde dead

1. The actions of Poole and the servants — e.g. the servants huddle together in fear, which suggests that something is wrong. This creates a tense atmosphere as it makes the reader think that something bad is going to happen. Stevenson's description of London — e.g. the personification of the moon "lying on her back" suggests that the natural order has been corrupted, which creates an eerie atmosphere.
2. Jekyll hasn't been seen for days and they hear Hyde's voice behind the door. They are worried about Jekyll's safety.
3. E.g. This creates a sense of mystery. The reader does not know where Jekyll is, or if Hyde has killed him.
4. E.g. He is afraid that Jekyll might be dead.
5. E.g. The narrator explains that the following chapters will reveal the mystery of Jekyll and Hyde, which makes the reader keen to read on.
Task: Here are some points you might have included:
  • Jekyll's house: "the pleasantest room in London" / "warmed (after the fashion of a country house) by a bright, open fire" / "costly cabinets of oak"
  • Hyde's house: "furnished with luxury and good taste" / "the little room in Soho" / "A good picture hung upon the walls"
  • Jekyll's lab: "there is a chimney which is generally smoking" / "the tables laden with chemical apparatus" / "light falling dimly through the foggy cupola"
  • Soho: "dismal quarter" / "a dingy street" / "ragged children huddled in the doorways"

Page 10: Dr Lanyon's Narrative
Lanyon's letter reveals the truth

1. E.g. The letter sounds very urgent and panicked, so Lanyon doesn't feel that he can refuse.
2. E.g. Lanyon dislikes Hyde when he first meets him. He explains that Hyde's actions "struck me, I confess, disagreeably".
3. E.g. It suggests the potion could be supernatural.
4. a) E.g. "he reeled, staggered, clutched at the table and held on"
   b) E.g. "my mind submerged in terror."
   c) E.g. "I ask myself if I believe it, and I cannot answer."
5. E.g. It increases the reader's feeling of suspense, as Lanyon does not describe what he saw, but only his own horror and disbelief.
Task: Here are some points you might have included if you sympathise with Jekyll:
  • He is desperate. He writes to Lanyon: "if you fail me tonight, I am lost". This shows he is in urgent need of help.
  • He is clearly troubled, telling Lanyon that he has "extreme distress of mind". This shows how severely he has been affected by his experiences, which makes the reader pity him.
Here are some points you might have included if you don't sympathise with Jekyll:
  • He doesn't mind that he's putting Lanyon in a difficult position. He suggests that what he asks Lanyon to do might be considered "dishonourable". This shows he puts his own need before Lanyon.

• He shows off to Lanyon. He uses boastful language like "you who have derided your superiors — behold!" This suggests he is revelling in showing Lanyon the identity of Hyde, which makes him less sympathetic.

Page 11: Henry Jekyll's Full Statement of the Case
Jekyll's letter explains everything

1. The statements should be numbered 3, 4, 1, 5, 6, 2, 7.
2. a) E.g. "the worst of all my faults was a certain impatient gaiety of disposition"
   b) E.g. "Many a man would have even emblazoned such irregularities as I was guilty of"
   c) E.g. "fond of the respect of the wise and good"
3. He wanted to separate man's dual nature.
4. E.g. He sees Hyde as "natural" and as a part of himself. Hyde is more pure and less divided than Jekyll.

Page 12: Henry Jekyll's Full Statement of the Case
Jekyll loses control of Hyde and kills himself

1. a) E.g. "I felt younger, lighter, happier in my body"
   b) E.g. "in an hour of moral weakness, I once again compounded and swallowed the transforming draught."
2. E.g. This suggests that Hyde is becoming more powerful, and Jekyll has lost control of him.
3. E.g. They make the reader see Hyde as an evil being, which might lead them to fear him.
4. E.g. He is horrified, and cries with "remorse". He vows to "redeem the past" and spend his time helping others.
5. E.g. Yes, because Hyde has a completely different personality to Jekyll and Jekyll dislikes Hyde's crimes, so he cannot be held responsible for Hyde's actions. **Or** e.g. No, because Jekyll controls when he becomes Hyde and appears to enjoy being Hyde. This suggests he is as guilty of the crimes as Hyde.
Task: You should have made a flowchart with arrows and labels showing various events in Jekyll's life. Here are some points you might have included:
  • Jekyll decides to invent a potion to separate the good and bad sides of himself.
  • When he drinks the potion, he initially thinks he's been successful, but then realises that he hasn't managed to rid himself of all of his negative qualities.
  • He wakes up one morning and realises that he's accidentally turned into Hyde.
  • He decides not to take the potion any more, but then gives in to temptation and takes it again.
  • He feels sickened by Hyde's murder of Carew.
  • He runs out of an important ingredient in the potion.
  • He knows he will become Hyde permanently, so he writes a letter explaining what's happened.
  • Jekyll kills himself.

Page 13: Skills Focus — Using Quotes

1. a - good, b - bad, c - good, d - bad, e - bad
2. Good quote usage: a) and d) [relevant and well embedded]
   Bad quote usage: b) [too long], c) [irrelevant] and e) [not embedded]
3. You could have rewritten the examples as follows:
   b) E.g. Hyde's brutal nature is shown when he breaks out "like a madman."
   c) E.g. Utterson is shocked by Hyde's appearance, regarding him as "hardly human".
   e) After Hyde disappears, Jekyll comes "out of seclusion" and returns to society.

Answers

Answers

Page 14: Skills Focus — P.E.E.D.

1. a) The Develop is missing. E.g. The way Jekyll feels the need to suppress his real self encourages the reader to sympathise with him.
   b) The Point is missing. E.g. In the novella, Stevenson uses language to create an unsettling atmosphere.
   c) The Explain is missing. E.g. The image of Jekyll's soul being ill suggests that witnessing the transformation was so horrifying that it corrupted the very core of his being.

Section Two — Characters

Pages 15-17: Henry Jekyll & Edward Hyde

1. a) E.g. "It is one of those affairs that cannot be mended by talking."
   b) E.g. "fond of the respect of the wise and good among my fellow-men."
   c) E.g. "he had always been known for charities"
2. E.g. Jekyll believes that there are two sides to human nature: a good side and a bad side. He states that "man is not truly one, but truly two."
3. E.g. Jekyll shows his ambitious character through his desire to be the first to separate the good and evil sides of man. His ambition is demonstrated when he experiments on himself in spite of the "infinite risk of death".
4. E.g. Jekyll's description of the pain he suffered because of his decisions makes the reader sympathise with him. For example, he says he was "racked" by the "horror of being Hyde".
5. b) E.g. Hyde was worried that he would get a bad reputation.
   c) E.g. Hyde was frightened of being caught.
   d) E.g. Hyde wanted to hurt and upset Jekyll. / Hyde has no respect for religious faith.
6. E.g. Jekyll has tried to live a good life and keep his evil side in check, so it is less fully developed.
7. E.g. This creates a sense of mystery. The reader never learns what Hyde really looks like, which makes him seem more frightening.
8. E.g. "I had taken a loathing to my gentleman at first sight." / "I saw that Sawbones turn sick and white with the desire to kill him" / "loathing and fear with which Mr Utterson regarded him."
9. E.g. The fact that Hyde gets physically bigger reflects how he is becoming more powerful, and that the evil side of Jekyll's nature is able to dominate the good side.
10. E.g. Jekyll is described as "handsome" and "well-made", whereas Hyde is "deformed". This makes Jekyll's appearance seem much more appealing than Hyde's.
11. E.g. The relationship is unequal. Jekyll cares about Hyde and feels responsible for him, but Hyde does not care about Jekyll.
12. E.g. Jekyll initially feels "happier" when he is Hyde, but he develops a hatred for Hyde as the story progresses. Jekyll says he "hated and feared" Hyde after Carew's murder.
13. E.g. Jekyll says that Hyde would have "ruined" himself in order to destroy Jekyll, showing that Hyde wishes him harm.
14. E.g. No, because while Hyde is described as "pure evil", Jekyll is a mixture of good and evil. Jekyll shows that he is not a virtuous character when he gives in to temptation and continues to drink the potion after Carew's murder.

Task: Here are some points that you might have included:
- In the extract, Lanyon can't explain his disgust for Hyde.
  - Lanyon's feelings = "idiosyncratic, personal distaste".
  - Lanyon thinks disgust is irrational, makes reader wonder why Hyde inspires such strong feelings, so adds to his mystery.
  - Other characters (e.g. Enfield) can't explain their dislike for Hyde clearly either.

- Hyde doesn't voice his own views.
  - Most other major characters narrate some events, but Hyde doesn't.
  - No insight into Hyde's motivations, so seems more mysterious.
  - Hyde's lack of narrative voice means the reader never understands him and can't sympathise with him.
- Hyde is often associated with darkness / fog.
  - When Hyde murders Carew, "a fog rolled over the city".
  - Darkness / fog often obscure Hyde from other characters' view — emphasises mystery around him.
  - Darkness emphasises Hyde's evil nature, making him seem more frightening to the reader.

Page 18: Gabriel Utterson

1. E.g. tolerant, likeable, reserved
   Any relevant quotes, e.g. "inclined to help rather than reprove." (tolerant) / "somehow lovable" (likeable) / "scanty and embarrassed in discourse" (reserved)
2. E.g. He is unable to believe the truth about Jekyll and Hyde. Instead of suspecting there is a supernatural cause, he comes up with rational explanations for the novella's events.
3. a) E.g. "If it came to a trial, your name might appear."
   b) E.g. "the man seems hardly human!"
   c) E.g. "he was perhaps relieved to be denied admittance"
4. E.g. Yes, in this chapter, he orders Poole to smash the door down so he can confront Hyde and learn the truth. His commanding behaviour and powerful actions show his bravery.

Page 19: Dr Hastie Lanyon

1. a) E.g. "he sprang up from his chair and welcomed him with both hands"
   b) E.g. "unscientific balderdash"
   c) E.g. "I shall never recover"
2. E.g. Lanyon and Jekyll used to be close, but ten years ago they stopped being friends when Jekyll "became too fanciful".
3. E.g. Lanyon's language is methodical and restrained. He uses few adverbs and doesn't describe events in detail. Jekyll is less concise and uses more figurative language, like "plentiful springs of distress".
4. E.g. Lanyon dies because of the "shock" of seeing Hyde transform into Jekyll.

Exam Practice:
Your answer should have an introduction, several paragraphs developing different ideas and a conclusion.
You may have covered some of the following points:
- In the extract, Lanyon is presented as the opposite of Jekyll. For example, he dismisses Jekyll's experiments as "unscientific balderdash". Lanyon's disapproval of work that falls outside the normal bounds of science is therefore contrasted with Jekyll's keenness to embrace it. Lanyon and Jekyll's differences reflect the growing divisions in the scientific community of Victorian society. Many Victorian scientists rejected new scientific theories such as evolution, which led to disagreements similar to that between Lanyon and Jekyll.
- In this extract, Stevenson presents Lanyon as a judgemental character. When he discusses why he and Jekyll are no longer friends, he claims that Jekyll "began to go wrong, wrong in mind". This shows that, although he had no clear knowledge of what Jekyll was doing, he discounted his research as madness. Lanyon is reluctant to change this judgement; he later clings to the idea that a "cerebral disease" is the cause of Jekyll's behaviour.

Answers

- Ultimately, Stevenson presents Lanyon as a victim of Jekyll's experiments. In his letter, Lanyon states that "the deadliest terror sits by me at all hours". Here, Stevenson uses the word "deadliest" to emphasise the idea that the impact of Hyde's transformation on Lanyon is so great that the shock is going to kill him. This causes the reader to sympathise with Lanyon because he is unable to cope with the fact that everything he believes in has been proven wrong.

Page 20: Mr Enfield & Poole

1. Enfield: Utterson's friend and relative. He is the first character to discuss Hyde and reveal his evil nature. Poole: Jekyll's butler. He supplies Utterson with information throughout the novella, e.g. Jekyll's reclusive behaviour in 'The Last Night'.
2. E.g. "make his name stink from one end of London to the other." / "I am ashamed of my long tongue."
3. E.g. This suggests that Enfield, like many of the other characters, is secretive about his behaviour.
4. E.g. Poole shows genuine concern for Jekyll in 'The Last Night', and tries to save him from Hyde.
5. E.g. It shows that his social status is lower than that of the other characters. It also makes it seem as though he respects the gentlemen in the novella.

Page 21: Skills Focus — Making Links

1. a) E.g. Lanyon. He chooses to stay with Hyde because he's curious about what Hyde will show him.
    b) E.g. Guest. He doesn't press Utterson for more information, even though the handwriting is curiously similar to Jekyll's.
2. Hyde: E.g. His uncivilised behaviour is shown through his use of violence. Examples — He "trampled calmly over" a young girl. / He murders Carew.
    Utterson: E.g. He thinks reputation is important. Examples — He protects Jekyll's reputation by not naming him when he talks to Enfield. / He worries that at Hyde's trial, Jekyll's "name might appear".
    Jekyll: E.g. His wish to appear respectable leads to secrecy. Examples — He refuses to tell Utterson anything about Hyde when questioned. / He slams the window down in front of Utterson and Enfield when he begins to transform.

Page 22: Practice Questions

Your answers should have an introduction, several paragraphs developing different ideas and a conclusion. You may have covered some of the following points:

1.
    - In the extract, Stevenson presents Jekyll and Hyde's relationship as hostile. Jekyll claims that he "hated and feared" the idea of the "brute" inside him. The word "brute" suggests that Jekyll views Hyde as a savage creature rather than a human being, which emphasises his hatred. Here, Stevenson could have been making a reference to Darwinism. By suggesting that Hyde is less evolved than the other characters, Stevenson emphasises the difference between Hyde and Jekyll and helps to explain the hostility between them.
    - Stevenson shows that Jekyll's feelings towards Hyde differ from Hyde's feelings towards Jekyll. In the final chapter, Jekyll uses father-son terminology when discussing his relationship with Hyde. He states that he "had more than a father's interest" in Hyde, whereas Hyde had "more than a son's indifference" towards Jekyll. This suggests that, as Hyde's creator, Jekyll has a desire to protect Hyde. By contrast, Hyde wants freedom from Jekyll. This struggle persists throughout the novella, creating tension for the reader.

- Throughout most of the novella, Jekyll and Hyde's relationship is mysterious. In 'Dr Jekyll was Quite at Ease', Jekyll states that he has "a very great interest in poor Hyde." Jekyll's language creates suspense, as the reader is left guessing why Jekyll has such an "interest" in someone as despicable as Hyde. This secret is maintained until the very end of the novella, which adds to the mystery of Jekyll and Hyde's relationship.

2. a)
    - In the extract, Utterson is presented as a serious character. For example, one of the first things that the reader is told about Utterson is that his face "was never lighted by a smile". This gives the impression that Utterson is a grave character who has few pleasures in life. By giving this description of Utterson in the first sentence of the novella, Stevenson could be suggesting that, like the reader, this is the first impression the characters have of Utterson when they meet him.
    - In the extract, Utterson is shown to live a strict lifestyle. For example, he "enjoyed the theatre" but has not visited one for twenty years. This implies that Utterson has strong will-power as, despite being aware of the pleasures of life, he actively suppresses them and lives a strict lifestyle. Utterson's restrained nature mirrors the lifestyle of typical Victorian gentlemen, who were expected to avoid sinful or indulgent behaviour.
    - Stevenson presents Utterson as a sociable character in this extract. The reader is told that Utterson's walks with Enfield are the "chief jewel of each week". By using the word "jewel", with its associations with beauty and expense, to apply to something free (like a walk), Stevenson emphasises how precious and valuable the walks are to both characters. This implies to the reader that Utterson highly values his relationship with Enfield. This metaphor contrasts with earlier descriptions of Utterson, as he is often described as cold and unsociable.

2. b)
    - Lanyon finds Hyde's presence disturbing but struggles to explain why. In his letter, Lanyon states that there was "something seizing, surprising and revolting" about Hyde. Here, Lanyon's vague language makes Hyde seem more mysterious and threatening to the reader. Other characters use similarly vague language to describe their reactions to Hyde, suggesting that they also find it difficult to express their feelings about him.
    - Stevenson uses the novella's multiple narrative viewpoints to emphasise the hatred that many characters feel for Hyde. He structures the novella so that it contains a series of narratives from the perspectives of Enfield, Utterson and Lanyon that describe Hyde negatively. This accumulation of negative opinions makes the characters' hatred of Hyde seem stronger. Near the end of the story, Hyde is described in more positive terms by Jekyll, but because the reader has learned so much about Hyde's true nature from several different sources, this description does not change their opinion.
    - Contrary to the rest of the characters, Jekyll's initial reaction to Hyde is positive. When he sees Hyde in the mirror after his first transformation, Jekyll states that he felt "a leap of welcome". The use of the word "leap" emphasises Jekyll's excitement as it seems as if he is unable to control his excitement. Jekyll's actions would have been particularly shocking for a Victorian reader, who lived in a very religious society, as Jekyll's positive attitude towards Hyde (who is the personification of his inner evil) would have been viewed as sinful.

3.
- In the extract, Jekyll treats temptation as an instinct. For example, Jekyll describes the temptations that he gives in to as Hyde as "appetites", suggesting that temptation is a natural instinct, similar to hunger. This implies that Jekyll believes he must give in to sin in order to sustain himself. This presentation of temptation as an instinct mirrors Evangelical Christian teachings that were common in Victorian England. Evangelicals believed that all people are naturally sinful, so would sympathise with Jekyll's ongoing struggle against the temptation to commit sin.
- In the extract, Stevenson uses narrative form to reveal how powerful an impact temptation has on Jekyll. In Jekyll's letter, Stevenson discusses Jekyll's inner struggle with temptation using a first-person narrative, which allows the reader greater insight into how far Jekyll believes temptation to be responsible for his actions. This narrative style encourages the reader to sympathise with Jekyll's inability to resist temptation by making his suffering and struggles clear.
- Utterson is presented as a restrained character who resists temptation. For example, the reader is told that, despite enjoying the theatre, Utterson "had not crossed the doors of one for twenty years". The revelation that Utterson can resist such a harmless temptation for such a long time demonstrates his moderate nature and the strength of his desire not to give in to temptation. Utterson's ability to resist temptation contrasts with Jekyll, whose behaviour is influenced by his inability to resist temptation.

4.
- In this extract, Jekyll is presented as a secretive character. For example, when he begins to transform, Jekyll immediately closes the window to prevent Utterson and Enfield from discovering his secret. The closure of the window symbolises him shutting his friends out of his life so they don't learn the truth. Stevenson uses closed windows and doors as symbols for Jekyll's secrecy elsewhere in the novella, such as when Poole has to break down the locked cabinet door in 'The Last Night' to uncover Jekyll's secret.
- Towards the end of the novella, Stevenson presents Jekyll as a hypocritical character. For example, when he discusses the sins that Hyde has committed, Jekyll concludes that it was "Hyde alone" who was "guilty", showing that Jekyll is denying responsibility for the crimes that he committed while he was Hyde. This hypocrisy encourages the reader to condemn Jekyll rather than feel sorry for him.
- In 'Henry Jekyll's Full Statement of the Case', Jekyll is revealed to be obsessed with his reputation. In the letter, Jekyll admits that he created Hyde because he had an "imperious desire" to appear virtuous in public. In this image, the word "imperious" makes Jekyll's "desire" seem like an arrogant and powerful ruler who controls Jekyll's actions. Jekyll's obsession with his reputation mirrors the concerns of many Victorian gentlemen; like Jekyll, they often tried to repress their desires in order to protect their reputations.

Section Three — Context and Themes

Page 23: Life in Victorian Britain

1. true, false, true, true
2. E.g. There are lots of "ragged children" in doorways, and the streets are described as "dingy".
3. a) E.g. Utterson drinks gin to "mortify a taste for vintages".
   b) E.g. Jekyll creates Hyde so that he can sin without his reputation suffering.
   c) E.g. Hyde is blackmailed into giving the girl's family £100.

4. E.g. He felt this caused a lot of problems. Jekyll keeps his immoral behaviour secret by creating Hyde. This leads to his eventual death, suggesting Stevenson was not in favour of keeping immoral behaviour secret.

Page 24: Reputation

1. E.g. "If it came to a trial, your name might appear" / "If your master has fled or is dead, we may at least save his credit." / "I begin to fear it is disgrace".
2. E.g. This passage shows that Jekyll is obsessed with his reputation. He admits to having "irregularities", and says that he "concealed" them from respectable society out of shame. This shows that he must use false appearances to maintain his reputation.
3. E.g. Hyde (the evil side of Jekyll) grows stronger as a result of Jekyll's attempts to maintain a good reputation — this suggests that Stevenson views the Victorian obsession with reputation as dangerous.
4. E.g. Yes, because he creates a being who can help him indulge his evil desires. This allows him to behave immorally whilst still protecting his reputation, which suggests that reputation is more important to him than morality.

Page 25: Secrecy

1. Jekyll — e.g. He refuses to tell Utterson about his links to Hyde. / "It is one of those affairs that cannot be mended by talking."
   Lanyon — e.g. In his letter, he doesn't say what Jekyll told him after the transformation. / "What he told me in the next hour, I cannot bring my mind to set on paper."
   Utterson — e.g. He doesn't speak to Hyde about his concerns over Jekyll's will. / "But he kept his feelings to himself".
2. a) E.g. "Let us make a bargain never to refer to this again."
   b) E.g. "If it came to a trial, your name might appear."
3. E.g. Like Utterson, the reader is trying to solve the mystery throughout the novella. Stevenson therefore creates suspense for the reader by only revealing the truth in the final chapters.
4. E.g. Characters often lock things to keep secrets secure. For example, Jekyll locks himself in his cabinet when he can no longer control his transformations.
Task: You should have written your paragraphs from Jekyll's point of view. Here are some points that you might have included in your first paragraph:
- At first, he wanted to protect his social reputation.
- Later, he felt shame and remorse for Hyde's actions.
- Gentlemen generally avoid gossip, so it would have seemed strange to talk about it.
Here are some points that you might have included in your second paragraph:
- It meant he couldn't ask for help. Had he told another scientist like Lanyon he might have been saved from death.
- After the murder of Carew, it was too late to tell Utterson the truth and confess that Hyde was part of him.
- He had to become reclusive in order to avoid people seeing him transforming into Hyde. This defeated the point of being seen as socially reputable and respectable.

Answers

Pages 26-27: Dual Nature of Man

1. a) E.g. "man is not truly one, but truly two."
   b) E.g. "the two natures that contended in the field of my consciousness"
   c) E.g. "Edward Hyde, alone in the ranks of mankind, was pure evil."
2. E.g. Jekyll states that the experiment might have produced "an angel instead of a fiend" if he had been less sinful.
3. E.g. Evil is shown to be more powerful because Hyde eventually becomes stronger than Jekyll, and Jekyll ends up killing himself.
4. E.g. No, because Jekyll says that after the experiment, he "was still the old Henry Jekyll", which suggests that he doesn't manage to completely separate his two sides.
5. E.g. Stevenson contrasts the "blistered" side door with the "wealth" of the front door of Jekyll's house. This contrast emphasises the difference between the respectable way Jekyll wants to be perceived and his evil side.
6. Events that are civilised — e.g. Jekyll hosts a dinner. / Utterson decides not to read Lanyon's letter.
   Events that are uncivilised — e.g. Hyde murders Carew. / Hyde annotates a Bible with "startling blasphemies."
7. E.g. "he broke out in a great flame of anger" / "Mr Hyde broke out of all bounds and clubbed him." / "he was trampling his victim under foot"
8. E.g. Jekyll 'wears' Hyde "like a thick cloak" to conceal his true nature. This simile shows that a person's nature and appearance don't always match.
9. E.g. Stevenson gives Jekyll a pleasant appearance with "every mark of capacity and kindness", which suggests that he is good. Hyde, however, has a repulsive appearance. His inner evil is shown through his face, which has "Satan's signature" on it.

Task: Various answers are possible, e.g.
   - Jekyll — 4. He enjoys committing immoral acts without having to suffer the consequences. However, he isn't entirely evil because he is charitable and does show remorse for some of Hyde's actions.
   - Utterson — 2. He is a loyal, trustworthy friend to Jekyll. However, he isn't completely good because he sometimes behaves in an unfriendly way. The fact that he's so drawn to Hyde might also suggest that he's drawn to the dark side of human nature that Hyde represents.

Pages 28-29: Science and Religion

1. Christian, Darwin, apes, controversial, origin, primitive
2. E.g. Yes, because Utterson says that "Jekyll had several times expressed a great esteem" for the Bible, which suggests that Jekyll respects the Bible and values religion.
3. E.g. Utterson — "though he enjoyed the theatre, had not crossed the doors of one for twenty years."
4. E.g. Stevenson compares Hyde to an animal when he describes his fury as "ape-like" and "like a monkey". By describing Hyde in this way, Stevenson suggests that Hyde is a primitive creature, and less evolved than humans, who themselves evolved from apes.
5. true, true, false, true
6. E.g. Lanyon believes in traditional science. He views Jekyll's experiments as "unscientific" because Jekyll focuses on the "mystic".
7. E.g. That science can be dangerous. In 'Dr. Lanyon's Narrative', Lanyon uses words such as "blood-red" and "volatile" to suggest that the ingredients in Jekyll's experiment are unsafe and could cause harm.
8. E.g. Hyde's transformation proves that Jekyll's science is real, which challenges Lanyon's sceptical attitude to Jekyll's experiments.

9. E.g. Yes, because Jekyll wanted to split his dual nature through his experiments. Instead, he created a creature who was evil, but he remained both good and evil. **Or** e.g. No, because he wanted to create someone who would allow him to be evil while maintaining his own respectable reputation. Hyde allowed him to do this.

Exam Practice:
Your answer should have an introduction, several paragraphs developing different ideas and a conclusion.
You may have covered some of the following points:
   - In this extract, Stevenson presents religion as important to Jekyll through the way he "lifted his clasped hands to God" out of "gratitude" that he was able to transform back successfully. This suggests that Jekyll views God as having power over him, including the ability to prevent him from changing back. However, Jekyll's attempts to separate the two sides of himself go against God and religion, which shows that he does not view God as all-powerful and does not fear God's power enough to let it limit his experiments.
   - Throughout the novella, Stevenson uses religious imagery to highlight Hyde's evil nature. For example, Jekyll refers to Hyde as a "child of Hell". The use of the word "child" suggests that Hyde was born in Hell and is therefore inherently evil. This imagery would have been especially effective in the 19th century, as society was more religious than it is today. The imagery of Hell that is linked to Hyde would therefore have made the character more frightening for a Victorian reader.
   - Religion is important as a way for the characters to maintain their reputation. After Carew's murder, Jekyll becomes "distinguished for religion", and in the final chapter, Jekyll himself says that this was as "penitence" for the murder. Doing religious works is his way of atoning for Carew's murder, almost as if he is seeking God's forgiveness for his part in Hyde's actions.

Page 30: Skills Focus — Writing about Context

1. a) You should have underlined: In Victorian Britain, poor areas were often associated with immorality, as they were home to businesses such as brothels and gin parlours. Wealthy areas appeared more respectable.
   b) You should have underlined: Shortly before *Jekyll and Hyde* was published, Charles Darwin published a theory about the evolution of mankind, explaining that apes were ancestors of humans. Darwin's theory contradicted Christian teachings about the origins of mankind at the time.
2. E.g. The sense of horror conveyed by the idea of hell would have been particularly effective to a Victorian reader as Christianity was an important part of Victorian society and people would have feared hell.

Page 31: Practice Questions

Your answers should have an introduction, several paragraphs developing different ideas and a conclusion. You may have covered some of the following points:
1.
   - In the extract, Stevenson presents science as horrifying through the vivid description of Hyde's transformation. One symptom of the transformation is "grinding in the bones". The use of an onomatopoeic verb like "grinding" allows the reader to almost 'hear' Hyde's transformation take place, which makes it seem particularly horrific and painful. This description encourages the reader to fear science and view it as a damaging and horrifying force.
   - Stevenson suggests that science is horrifying in this extract through the way it affects Jekyll's soul. When describing the impact his transformation had on him, Jekyll claims

that he felt a "horror of the spirit". This emphasises the horror of science as his transformation is shown to cause pain not only to his body, but also to his soul. The idea that this horror cannot be felt more strongly "at the hour of birth or death", arguably the most significant times of a person's life, confirms its dramatic effect on Jekyll.

- Stevenson presents science as horrifying through his description of Hyde, who is created as a result of scientific experimentation. In the last chapter of the novella, Jekyll describes his creation as "pure evil". The idea that science can overcome the dual nature of man by producing a completely evil being suggests that it has the potential to be used for sinister ends. Stevenson also uses Hyde to emphasise the horror of science through the repeated comparison between him and "Satan", which reinforces the suggestion that science is capable of bringing hellish creatures to life.

2.
- In the extract, secrecy is important as a means of creating intrigue. In his letter to Utterson, Jekyll says that he is being punished for something that he "cannot name". The use of the word "cannot" makes it seem as if Jekyll is physically unable to tell Utterson what he has done, rather than simply choosing not to, which makes the reader try to guess what he is being punished for. Jekyll feels compelled to secrecy to protect his reputation, as in Victorian times a reputation for immoral activity could lose a gentleman wealthy clients and lead to financial ruin. This heightens the intrigue around Jekyll, as it implies that his secret is scandalous enough to threaten his social position.
- Secrecy is important as a means of creating suspense at the climax of the novella. Stevenson maintains the secrecy surrounding Hyde's identity throughout the story, and therefore holds the reader in suspense until Poole breaks down the door of the cabinet, symbolically shattering Jekyll's wall of secrecy. Stevenson uses the symbol of the door elsewhere in the novella to indicate secrecy, such as when Utterson locks Lanyon's letter away in his safe rather than reading it, which creates suspense by making the reader anticipate the letter's contents.
- Stevenson uses form to demonstrate the importance of secrecy in the novella by giving the text elements of a detective story. The narrative of the first eight chapters follows Utterson as a 'detective' who is following clues and gathering information to solve the mystery. The secrecy of the other characters is therefore important as it thwarts his efforts. The link between secrecy and the form of the novella is also reflected in the fact that, like a detective story, the secret is only revealed at the end of the novella.

3.
- The struggle between good and evil is important in the novella as it creates conflict. When Jekyll discusses his internal struggle, he uses language related to division, such as the suggestion that there is a "deeper trench" inside of him. Here, Jekyll suggests that he has become physically torn apart by the opposing forces of good and evil. The struggle between Jekyll and Hyde represents the larger-scale struggle between God and the devil; to a Victorian reader with deep-seated religious beliefs, this may have been a more important aspect of the novella than it is to many modern readers.
- The tragic ending of the novella demonstrates the influence that the struggle between good and evil has in the story. At the end of the novella, Jekyll feels forced to commit suicide after he loses control of Hyde. The fact that Jekyll and Hyde both die could suggest that good and evil are evenly matched in their struggle. This outcome may imply that the struggle between good and

evil is ongoing; Stevenson may therefore be suggesting that people should be aware of it, hinting that it is an important part of the message he wanted to convey.
- The novella is structured in a way that means the reader only learns about the struggle between good and evil in the final chapter, suggesting it is not pivotal to the story. Instead, Utterson's investigation into Hyde's identity is the central focus of the majority of the novella. As such, the struggle between good and evil plays a relatively minor role compared to the mystery of Hyde's identity. Ultimately, the revelation that Jekyll and Hyde are two sides of the same person is likely to shock the reader more than the revelation that every man has both good and evil within him.

4. a)
- In this extract, having a good reputation is presented as important. When Enfield spreads rumours about Hyde, he regrets his behaviour, stating "I am ashamed of my long tongue". This emphasises the importance of reputation as Enfield resolves to refrain from spreading rumours in the future. By highlighting the importance of reputation, Stevenson could have been pointing out the hypocrisy of a society where reputation was prioritised over the truth.
- In this extract, reputation is shown to be an obsession of Utterson's. When talking about Jekyll, Utterson says, "if I do not ask you the name of the other party, it is because I know it already." Utterson speaks cautiously throughout this conversation. Even though he knows who Enfield is talking about, Utterson refuses to name Jekyll in order to protect Jekyll's reputation. The importance of reputation to Utterson is made more explicit in later chapters, such as when Utterson refuses to tell the police about Hyde's links to Jekyll in order to protect Jekyll's reputation.
- Stevenson highlights the relationship between reputation and appearances in the extract. Enfield refers to Hyde's "strong feeling of deformity" to justify his dislike for him. The close proximity between Enfield's description of Hyde and his personal dislike for Hyde suggests that the two are linked — Hyde's bad reputation seems to be caused in part by his deformed appearance. This link is reinforced later in the novella when Utterson compares Hyde's appearance to that of a caveman to justify his hatred for him.

4. b)
- In the first chapter, Enfield reveals that he understands the extent to which people will try to protect their name. After the young girl is trampled, Enfield warns Hyde that he will "make his name stink" if he doesn't compensate the girl's family. By using the word "stink", Enfield suggests that news of Hyde's bad reputation would spread across London like a bad smell, 'sickening' those who encountered it. The fact that the disreputable character of Hyde pays the money to the family suggests that even he has anxieties about his reputation, emphasising how important reputation is to the characters of the novella.
- In the final chapter, Jekyll admits that he is obsessed with his reputation. This obsession influences his nature; he states that, though he had a "gaiety of disposition", he had to maintain a "grave countenance". This shows that Jekyll's entire nature is shaped by his desire for a good reputation, emphasising its importance. Jekyll's obsession with his reputation mirrors the anxieties of many Victorian gentlemen, who understood the importance of reputation and feared losing their own.
- Stevenson suggests reputation is important by showing that characters care about others' reputations in addition to their own. For example, Utterson is keen to protect Jekyll's reputation. After Carew's murder, Utterson tells Jekyll "If it came to a trial, your name might appear."

This reveals Utterson's obsession with reputation as he prioritises Jekyll's reputation over justice for Hyde's victims. This may encourage the reader to criticise Utterson for his inability to look beyond his obsession with reputation and seek justice for Carew.

Section Four — The Writer's Techniques

Pages 32-33: Structure and Narrative

1. E.g. This violent event grabs the reader's attention. The unexplained aspects of the event, such as the identity of the man who signed the cheque, create a sense of mystery.
2. E.g. This maintains the mystery of Hyde's identity and his relationship with Jekyll.
3. a) E.g. Hyde murders Carew.
   b) E.g. It is revealed that Jekyll has been keeping secrets.
   c) E.g. Hyde overpowers Jekyll, who loses control of him.
4. E.g. Describing the events of the novella from multiple points of view makes the story more realistic and believable.
5. E.g. To make Hyde seem more mysterious by making it so that the reader never learns what Hyde is thinking.
6. E.g. It creates suspense. The earlier chapter suggests to the reader that the cause of Lanyon's death is mysterious but they have to wait until the later chapter for the mystery to be solved.
7. E.g. Lanyon's letter gives the reader information but it still has gaps. Jekyll's letter fills in the gaps, so it makes sense for it to come afterwards.
8. a) True: e.g. It includes the note from Jekyll.
   b) False: e.g. He can't bring himself to write everything.
   c) True: e.g. He says that his mind was "submerged in terror".
9. E.g. By giving Jekyll his own narrative, Stevenson is able to tell the full story of Jekyll's transformation, which solves the mystery for the reader. / Using Jekyll's own words helps the reader to sympathise with him, which strengthens Stevenson's message that everyone has good and evil within them.

Pages 34-35: Setting and Symbolism

1. frightening, mazes, lost, setting, evil
2. E.g. It makes the story more frightening. Supernatural events seem more believable when they're set in a real place like London.
3. E.g. Soho, which the narrator describes as "dismal", was one of the least respectable areas of Victorian London. The area is used to emphasise Hyde's wicked and sinful nature to the reader.
4. a) E.g. Fog is used to make the novella's events more sinister and mysterious. For example, a thick fog appears when Carew is murdered by Hyde.
   b) E.g. The fog represents the extent of Jekyll's secrecy. He has hidden the truth about Hyde so deeply that the fog surrounds him inside his house.
5. E.g. The intrusion into the private space where Jekyll has hidden himself symbolises the fact that Jekyll's secret will come to light.
6. E.g. The moon is shining brightly when Carew is murdered. / In 'The Last Night', the moon is "lying on her back".
7. You should have ticked the first, third and fourth boxes.
8. E.g. Utterson recognises the cane as a present that he gave to Jekyll, which associates it with civilised society. The fact that Hyde uses the cane to kill Carew suggests that civilised men like Jekyll can commit sin.
9. E.g. The mirror is used to symbolise Jekyll's dual nature. The fact that Jekyll can see Hyde in the mirror suggests that he has evil inside him.

Pages 36-38: Language and Dialogue

1. vivid, simile, aggression, horror
2. E.g. This wordplay makes it seem as though Utterson is being light-hearted. This is out of character, as his language is usually serious and factual.
3. a) "You do not understand my position"
   b) "he is safe, he is quite safe"
   c) "Your unworthy and unhappy friend"
4. E.g. In the earlier chapter, Lanyon uses long sentences and descriptive language. In the later chapter, his speech is disjointed and contains lots of short phrases, like "life has been pleasant; I like it; yes, sir". This makes his speech fragmented and less coherent.
5. E.g. He repeats "very low" and sighs, which suggests that he is resigned. His repetition of "no" and "dare not" make him seem fearful. His tone is also regretful when he says he can't go down to see Utterson.
6. E.g. "Yes, sir, he do indeed."
   Any valid explanation, e.g. This language shows that Poole is less educated than the gentlemen and that he is from a lower social class.
7. E.g. Hyde's language is aggressive and blunt. He accuses Utterson of lying, which Utterson finds shocking and rude. This suggests that Hyde is uncivilised and hostile.
8. E.g. "Tut-tut" is an understated reaction. This suggests that like many Victorian gentlemen, he is expected to have stable emotions.
9. E.g. This creates a contrast with the vivid description of the horrific events. The horrific events therefore seem even more shocking to the reader.
10. Metaphor: e.g. "a great flame of anger". This makes it seem as though Hyde's anger is so fierce that it can't be controlled.
    Metaphor: e.g. "Mr Hyde broke out of all bounds". This makes it seem as though Hyde has broken free of the chains that restrain him.
    Personification: "mournful reinvasion of darkness". The way the darkness is 'reinvading' makes it seem like an army. The word "mournful" suggests that the 'army' is creeping stealthily, and possibly unwillingly.
    Personification: e.g. "the wind was continually charging and routing these embattled vapours". This makes it sound as though the wind and fog are opposing armies, which gives the impression that London is in turmoil.
11. E.g. Carew's murder. This emphasises Hyde's violent nature, encouraging the reader to fear him.
12. E.g. To suggest to the reader that Hyde is so evil that the characters are unable to describe him directly and must rely on comparisons.
13. E.g. Jekyll calls himself "a creature eaten up and emptied by fever". The idea that Jekyll has been consumed makes it seem as though he is a victim and creates sympathy for him.

Exam Practice:
   Your answer should have an introduction, several paragraphs developing different ideas and a conclusion.
   You may have covered some of the following points:
   • In the extract, Utterson shows his morality by resisting the temptation to read Lanyon's letter. Instead, Utterson places it "in the inmost corner of his private safe." The word "inmost" emphasises how deeply the letter has been locked away, literally in the safe and more metaphorically in Utterson's mind, demonstrating his dedication to keeping its contents secret. The fact that Utterson is tempted to open the letter develops the theme of the dual nature of man; it shows that even those who appear respectable have the potential to behave immorally.

Answers

Answers

- Utterson's moral nature is implied by his first name, Gabriel. In the Bible, Gabriel is an angel who usually serves as God's messenger. As such, by naming Utterson after one of God's angels, Stevenson could be implying that Utterson is a moral character. The link between Utterson and the angel Gabriel would have stood out particularly clearly to readers in the 19th century, when Christianity had a particularly strong influence over everyday life.
- Stevenson shows that Utterson is a moral character through Utterson's consistently good treatment of others. The reader is told that he "never marked a shade of change in his demeanour" towards other people. By referring to Utterson's "shade", Stevenson suggests that the 'colour' of Utterson's morality is so strong that it cannot fade. This consistently good treatment of people is reinforced through Utterson's constant desire to protect Jekyll's reputation from being damaged by his secret.

Page 39: 'Jekyll and Hyde' as a Gothic Novel

1. There is often a character who is an 'outsider' in society. — E.g. Hyde is seen as repulsive by others.
   Science is often presented as unsettling. — E.g. Jekyll's experiments are unnatural and violent.
   There is often an evil villain. — E.g. Jekyll describes Hyde as "pure evil."
   The settings are usually mysterious. — E.g. Victorian London is presented as dark and foggy.
2. a) E.g. The novella is set in London, England.
   b) E.g. Hyde is described as "deformed" and "ugly".
   c) E.g. There aren't any major female characters in *Jekyll and Hyde*.
3. E.g. Yes, because it includes many important features of a traditional Gothic novel. The ways in which Stevenson challenges tradition are fairly small. **Or** e.g. no, because Stevenson challenges the traditional form of a Gothic novel by having a familiar setting.
Task: You may have included the following points:
   - London would have been familiar to many readers, so the events would have been easier to imagine.
   - By setting the novella in a familiar place, Stevenson makes the events seem more terrifying than if they had taken place in a faraway location because it seems more likely that they could happen.
   - The familiar setting helps to convey information about his characters. For instance, many readers would have known that London had disreputable areas. Hyde is linked with these areas, so readers would have understood that Stevenson was trying to portray him in a negative light through this association.

Page 40: Skills Focus — Working with Extracts

1. It's from the start of Chapter Four. At the end of the last chapter, Utterson promises to carry out the instructions in Jekyll's will. Utterson is about to lead the police to Hyde's house.
2. E.g. It suggests that Hyde's temper has an animalistic ferocity that is not restrained by human conscience.
3. E.g. Carew's body is left "incredibly mangled", which suggests it has been severely damaged by the attack.
4. E.g. Shortly before Hyde meets Lanyon, he hits a woman in the face.

Page 41: Practice Questions

Your answers should have an introduction, several paragraphs developing different ideas and a conclusion. You may have covered some of the following points:

1. - In the extract, Stevenson uses nature to create a mysterious atmosphere. The moon is said to be "lying on her back as though the wind had tilted her". By suggesting that the moon has been physically moved by the wind, Stevenson implies that the natural world has become unstable. This creates a mysterious atmosphere because the reader is unsure what is causing this instability. The fog which lingers around Hyde's house in Soho also creates a mysterious atmosphere by making the true identity of its inhabitant seem more intriguing.
   - Stevenson creates a mysterious atmosphere through his description of Utterson's anxiety in this extract. On his way to Jekyll's house, Utterson feels "a crushing anticipation of calamity." The use of the verb "crushing" to describe Utterson's feelings suggests that he feels the physical weight of the terrible events to come. As Utterson is normally a rational and reserved character, this sense of premonition hints at supernatural events and adds to the mysterious atmosphere of the extract. Utterson's anxious desire to discover Hyde's identity throughout the story strengthens the mysterious mood of the novella by keeping the mystery surrounding Hyde at the forefront of the reader's mind.
   - Stevenson uses setting to create a mysterious atmosphere. The story is set in Victorian London, which is described as being "empty as a church". This impression of emptiness contradicts the nature of the real 19th-century London, which was bustling and often overcrowded. Stevenson therefore presents the reader with a setting that they know but cannot recognise, which creates a mysterious atmosphere by suggesting that something odd is occurring. The setting also contradicts Gothic form by not using a distant location. This heightens the novella's mystery by implying that it will not follow a predictable pattern.

2. - In the extract, science is presented as unnatural through the way the potion acts on Hyde as he transforms. Lanyon explains that his face turned black and his features "seemed to melt and alter". Blackening and melting are usually the effects of fire or extreme heat, so the fact that a potion can cause these changes makes Jekyll's scientific advances seem unnatural. The sense that Hyde is brought to life through an unnatural, sinister process may reflect the widespread feeling in Victorian Britain that the idea that science could create life was dangerous.
   - Stevenson suggests that science is unnatural through the potion's ability to affect identity itself. Jekyll claims that it was so powerful that it "shook the very fortress of identity". Describing identity as a "fortress" suggests that a person's nature is permanent and unchangeable, so the idea that the potion can change identity emphasises its unnatural power. The fact that Jekyll later loses control of the transformation highlights the extraordinary power of his 'unnatural' science.
   - Stevenson suggests that Jekyll's experiments are unnatural because they go against Christian teachings. Jekyll himself states that humans are "not truly one, but truly two", reflecting the idea taught by Evangelical Christians that even 'good' people are naturally sinful. Jekyll's attempt to extract the sinfulness from his character through his creation of Hyde may therefore have been considered unnatural by Evangelicals. This idea is reinforced through the way Hyde scribbles "blasphemies" on one of Jekyll's

Answers

religious texts; Jekyll's scientific creation appears to actively despise religious teachings.

3.
- Stevenson uses the setting of Jekyll's laboratory to create suspense. In the extract, Stevenson describes the theatre as "once crowded with eager students and now lying gaunt and silent". The emptiness creates a sense of unease as it emphasises how isolated Jekyll has become from society, and builds suspense as the reader is left to guess why Jekyll has chosen to hide himself away from his friends. The silence of Jekyll's laboratory and house emphasises how much he has changed since 'Dr Jekyll was Quite at Ease', in which he seemed sociable.
- The use of fog in the setting of this extract creates a sense of foreboding. The way the fog lies "thickly" inside Jekyll's laboratory creates a mysterious atmosphere by suggesting that some of his secrets may be deeply hidden from view. The sense of foreboding in the passage is heightened through the way the light still falls through the "foggy cupola", indicating that the light may yet illuminate Jekyll's secrets in future.
- Stevenson's use of London as a backdrop for the novella helps to create an unsettling atmosphere. In 'Search for Mr Hyde', London's streets are referred to as "labyrinths". This description brings to mind the feeling of being lost; it is as if Utterson is stuck inside a maze. During the 19th century, London expanded rapidly and large areas of slums were built with unplanned layouts. These areas would have felt unfamiliar and frightening to many readers, so Stevenson's representation of this aspect of London would have heightened the unsettling atmosphere.

4. a)
- Stevenson creates suspense in the extract through the way he delays the discovery of Jekyll's secret. The last paragraph of the extract is composed of two long sentences describing the route Utterson and Poole take to Jekyll's cabinet. These sentences slow down the pace of the narrative just before it seems likely that Jekyll's secret will be revealed, forcing the reader to wait in suspense for the discovery. The sense of delay is emphasised through Poole and Utterson's business-like manner; their urgency makes Stevenson's delay seem more frustrating to the reader.
- Suspense is also created through the description of the servants, who are "huddled together like a flock of sheep" out of fear. This gives the impression of the servants as helpless prey, which makes the reader wonder what 'predator' they are afraid of. The "hysterical whimpering" of the housemaid increases this anticipation; she is so terrified that she cannot speak properly.
- The characters' appeals to God at the start of the extract contribute to the suspense. Poole asks that "God grant there be nothing wrong", and Utterson replies with "Amen". These appeals to God show that the characters think that the situation is beyond human control. This makes the reader keen to discover why the characters believe themselves to be so powerless. The characters' pleas to God would have been particularly effective in conveying the seriousness of the situation to readers in the 19th century, when Christianity had a particularly strong influence over people's lives.

4. b)
- Stevenson uses structure to present the power that Jekyll's fear has over him. He structures the events of 'Incident at the Window' so that Jekyll thrusts down the window to shut out Utterson and Enfield immediately after agreeing to speak with them. This emphasises how suddenly and completely Jekyll's behaviour changes, which suggests that his fear of discovery is causing him to react instinctively

and is therefore dictating his actions. This creates suspense, as the reader wants to know the truth behind what is causing Jekyll's extreme fear.
- In the novella, Stevenson uses Jekyll's dialogue to reveal his fear. For example, in 'Incident at the Window', when Utterson asks his friend to come outside, Jekyll says "no, no, no, it is quite impossible". The repetition of "no" reinforces his certainty that he can't leave the house, which makes him seem paralysed by fear. Their glimpse of Jekyll's transformation makes Utterson and Enfield fearful by the end of this chapter, which makes fear seem almost contagious.
- Utterson responds to fear by trying to explain away mysterious events. For example, when Guest points out the similarity between Jekyll's handwriting and that of the murderer in 'Incident of the Letter', Utterson jumps to the conclusion that Jekyll must have forged the murderer's note, despite having no evidence to suggest this. This demonstrates Utterson's desire to comfort himself by thinking rationally. However, the fact that even Utterson, a lawyer used to weighing up evidence, draws unfounded conclusions emphasises to the reader just how much he, too, is affected by fear.

Section Five — Exam Buster

Page 42: Understanding the Question

1. b) <u>Explain how</u> the theme of <u>religion</u> is <u>presented</u> in *Jekyll and Hyde*.
   c) <u>Write about how</u> the <u>relationship</u> between <u>Jekyll</u> and <u>Hyde changes</u> throughout the novella.
   d) <u>How</u> is the theme of <u>reputation presented</u> in *Jekyll and Hyde*?
   e) <u>Explore</u> the <u>importance</u> of <u>secrecy</u> in *Jekyll and Hyde*.
   f) <u>Write about</u> the <u>importance</u> of <u>Utterson</u> in *Jekyll and Hyde*.
   g) <u>How</u> does Stevenson <u>create</u> a <u>fearful atmosphere</u> in the novella?

2. a - 3, b - 4, c - 2, d - 1, e - 5

Page 43: Making a Rough Plan

1. E.g. Stevenson uses animalistic language to describe Hyde's actions. / Hyde becomes violent easily. / Hyde enjoys causing others pain.

2. Pick your three most important points and put them in a sensible order. Write down a quote or an example from the text to back up each one.

Page 44: Making Links

1. Maintaining a good reputation is important. E.g. Utterson is more preoccupied with saving Jekyll's reputation than making sure Hyde is punished.
   A person's reputation can often disguise their real nature. E.g. Utterson is a respected gentleman, but has done "many ill things"
   The gentlemen are reluctant to spread rumours about others. E.g. Utterson warns Guest not to tell anyone about the letter that he has been shown.

2. E.g. If one of your points was 'Hyde becomes violent easily', and your evidence was that he tramples the little girl without being provoked, another example could be that "all of a sudden" he breaks out in anger and attacks Carew.

Answers

Page 45: Structuring Your Answer

1. Point: Lanyon disapproves of the nature of Jekyll's scientific experiments.
   Example: This is implied when Jekyll claims that Lanyon called his work "scientific heresies".
   Explanation: 'Heresy' can mean a belief or action that goes against the teachings of God, which might suggest that Lanyon considers Jekyll's experiments to be ungodly.
   Develop: Most Victorians were religious and believed that humans were created by God. As such, it is likely that Victorian readers would have shared Lanyon's belief that Jekyll's experiments were indecent.
2. a) E.g. Lanyon believes that Jekyll has gone "wrong in mind".
   b) E.g. Jekyll "hated and feared" Hyde.
3. Point: Stevenson uses animalistic language to describe Hyde's violent actions.
   Example: In 'Henry Jekyll's Full Statement of the Case', Stevenson says that Hyde had been "caged" and then came out "roaring" before murdering Carew.
   Explanation: This makes him sound savage and suggests that he commits violence on instinct.
   Development: This makes Hyde seem more dangerous, as he might not respond to reason and so he will be unpredictable.

Page 46: Introductions and Conclusions

1. Intro b) is better, e.g. Intro a) focuses on one way Stevenson creates a fearful atmosphere and begins to analyse it. It also includes information that isn't directly relevant to the question, as it discusses how Hyde's character appears to the reader.
2. E.g. The conclusion should focus on how Stevenson creates a fearful atmosphere, rather than on why the fearful atmosphere is important to the novella as a whole. It should provide a clear answer to the question.
Task: Your introduction and conclusion should both give a clear answer to the question. The introduction should include your main points, but no evidence. Your conclusion should summarise your argument and not include new points.

Page 47: Writing about Context

1. a-2, b-1, c-3
2. You should have underlined: "the hypocrisy that existed in the Victorian upper class" / "His behaviour reflects the pressures that many gentlemen were under in 19th-century society to maintain an air of respectability."
3. You could have included context as the Explain or Develop part of the paragraph. The context you wrote about should be relevant to your Point and linked to the Example.

Page 48: Linking Ideas and Paragraphs

1. E.g. The characters of Utterson and Enfield both ignore unpleasant realities. For example, Enfield talks about the trampled young girl in a matter-of-fact tone, and Utterson chooses not to read Lanyon's letter. This highlights their refusal to engage with anything scandalous or dishonourable. It also emphasises the important role that secrecy has in the novella.
2. You should have used the P.E.E.D. structure and included connecting words and phrases such as 'therefore' or 'which shows that' to link your ideas.
3. E.g. Stevenson also presents Hyde as violent when... / This idea is reinforced by...

Page 49: Marking Answer Extracts

1. 4-5: The answer makes a clear point that answers the question and brings in the wider themes of the novella. However, the point is not developed or analytical enough for it to be a 6-7 answer. There is limited reference to context, no analysis of Stevenson's language, and there are also some spelling errors.

Page 50: Marking Answer Extracts

1. a) 8-9: E.g. "this description creates a vivid image... attached to them indefinitely" — close and perceptive analysis of how Stevenson uses language
   "It also makes Lanyon seem very energetic... reserved." — insightful and critical personal response to the text
   b) 6-7: E.g. "In 'Dr Jekyll was Quite at Ease'... admit Utterson into his house." — thorough analysis of the effect of structure
   "his concern for Jekyll's reputation... doing the right thing" — thorough exploration of the context of the novella

Pages 51-52: Marking a Whole Answer

1. 8-9: E.g. The answer shows an insightful and critical personal response to the text. It makes a variety of interesting points and gives a thorough overview of how the dual nature of man is presented. There is close and perceptive analysis of language, for example in the fifth paragraph, which examines the effect of specific vocabulary.

Page 53: Skills Focus — Writing Well

1. As the novella progresses, <u>Jeckyll</u> [Jekyll] gradually realises that he can no longer control the "brute" inside him. This is shown when Jekyll transforms into Hyde without <u>drinkin</u> [drinking] the potion. Instead of allowing <u>hyde</u> [Hyde] to control him, Jekyll locks himself in his cabinet and <u>dyes</u> [dies]. His death is tragic<u>:</u> [,] which cause the reader to sympathise with him.
2. You could have rewritten the sentences as follows:
   a) Jekyll tries to repress his urges to protect his reputation.
   b) Stevenson's presentation of London gives the impression that it is threatening and dangerous.
   c) Lanyon's language is initially light-hearted, but becomes more serious in later chapters.
   d) Carew is presented as a likeable character who appears to be respected by others.

Page 54: Practice Questions

Your answers should have an introduction, several paragraphs developing different ideas and a conclusion. You may have covered some of the following points:

1. • The fast pace of the extract builds excitement. Stevenson uses short clauses, such as "Up went the axe again", to increase the pace of the action. This faster pace suggests that events are building to a climax, which escalates the feeling of drama. Stevenson uses violent, onomatopoeic verbs such as "crashed" and "burst" to highlight the noise and energy of Poole's efforts to break down the door, which also adds to the reader's anticipation of what lies behind the door.
   • Excitement is created in the novella as a whole through Stevenson's use of form. The mystery of Jekyll and Hyde's relationship, as well as Utterson's role as a detective-like figure, give the novella features of a detective story. The clues that Utterson finds about Hyde build anticipation as the reader is eager to learn the truth. This form also builds excitement because the reader is aware that there is likely to be a twist or big 'reveal' near the end of the story.

Answers

- Stevenson also uses settings to heighten the sense of excitement. The choice of London as the main setting of the novella would have increased suspense for 19th-century readers, many of whom would have been familiar with the "fallen clouds" of fog and the dark and mysterious streets of London that Stevenson describes. This would have increased excitement, as the disturbing events of the story would have seemed more realistic. A modern-day reader might find Stevenson's London mysterious and unfamiliar, which could also add to their sense of excitement.

2. a)
  - In the extract, the extent of Jekyll's suffering reveals the dangers of science. Jekyll claims that "no one has ever suffered such torments". The word "torments" suggests that Jekyll has been tortured by his experiments, which implies that science can be dangerous. Many Victorian readers would have expected Gothic novels to include an evil character, but in the novella, science aids in the creation of evil within an ordinary Victorian gentleman. This may have made science seem threatening to Victorian readers, because it has frightening, unintended results.
  - Stevenson demonstrates the dangers of science through the power it has over Jekyll. In the extract, Jekyll states that running out of the impure salt that makes his potion work has "severed" him from his "face and nature." The word "severed" suggests that there has been an irreversible split in his identity. Stevenson therefore reveals the dangers of science through its power to break down one's identity. This is also shown by the fact that Jekyll starts to refer to himself in the third person; he sees Henry Jekyll as a separate being.
  - In the extract, Jekyll's vivid language emphasises the destructive power that science can have. He states that "doom" is "closing on" himself and Hyde. Here, the word "doom" suggests that his experiments will inevitably lead to his death and highlights the idea that there can be no escape from his fate at this point. Stevenson therefore signals to the reader that Jekyll's recognition of the power and danger of science has replaced his earlier arrogance.

2. b)
  - Stevenson uses science in the novella to create conflict between characters. For example, the divisions between Jekyll and Lanyon originated from a dispute about Jekyll's experiments. Lanyon states that "Such unscientific balderdash... would have estranged Damon and Pythias." Here, Lanyon references a Greek legend about an extremely loyal friendship to show the extent of their conflict over the nature of science. Conflict between Lanyon's traditional science and Jekyll's "transcendental" science relates to conflict in Victorian society between people who believed Darwin's theory of evolution and those who believed that God created the Earth.
  - Science drives the events of the novella. For example, an "unknown impurity" allows Jekyll's potion to work but also makes it impossible to replicate. This means that, when the original potion runs out, Jekyll can no longer control Hyde and feels forced to kill himself; in this way, science is arguably responsible for his death. It is ironic that science encourages Jekyll to investigate the mystical, but it is actually lack of resources, which is a very mundane and material aspect of science, that causes his death.
  - Charles Darwin's theory of evolution is an element of science that is important to the text. Darwin stated that humans are just animals which have evolved from apes. Throughout the novella, Hyde is compared to an ape, so this suggests that he is less evolved and more animalistic

than Jekyll. The fact that Stevenson uses Hyde to explore the primitive aspects of Jekyll, who is a respectable gentleman, forces the reader to consider the idea that even the most civilised people have a savage side.

3.
  - In this extract, Jekyll's remorse makes him seem like a victim of his own actions. When vowing that he will never see Hyde again, he repeats the words "I swear to God". This repeated promise to make amends makes him seem desperate, particularly because oaths to God would have been taken very seriously in the strongly religious climate of Victorian Britain. Despite this remorse, however, some readers may not feel sympathy for Jekyll due to the "selfishness" that Utterson notes; Jekyll is more concerned about damage to his reputation than about the brutal murder of Carew.
  - Stevenson uses the structure of the novella to emphasise Jekyll's suffering. In the extract, Utterson says that Jekyll has a "feverish manner", which contrasts with his healthy appearance just two chapters before. In the final chapter, Jekyll notes that Hyde's power has "grown" with Jekyll's own "sickliness". Presenting Jekyll's declining health from two different narrative perspectives highlights his suffering, which encourages the audience to see him as a victim. Jekyll's role as a victim is emphasised by the first-person narrative Stevenson uses in the final chapter to vividly describe the pain and suffering Jekyll has experienced.
  - Jekyll is presented as a victim of Hyde. In the final chapter, Jekyll says that the "hideous images and sounds" of Carew's murder "swarmed against" him. The fact that Jekyll finds the memories of the murder "hideous" highlights his suffering as a result of Hyde's actions. The image of them 'swarming against' him reinforces this idea because it makes it seem like Jekyll is being physically attacked. Jekyll's defencelessness is also highlighted in 'The Last Night'; his dead body takes on the form of Hyde, showing how he has been overpowered.

4.
  - In the extract, Stevenson uses satanic descriptions to show the horror of Hyde's character. For example, Jekyll describes Hyde as "hellish". By using this description, Jekyll is suggesting that Hyde is so evil and horrifying that he is almost like a creature from hell. This comparison would have been particularly effective in a religious society like that of the Victorians. Imagery of heaven and hell would have been familiar to religious Victorians, so readers at the time would have felt the horror that Stevenson was conveying.
  - Jekyll uses imagery to convey the horror of his situation. In the extract, he claims that he was "a creature eaten up and emptied by fever". This personification of "fever" is particularly gruesome as it suggests that the fever is 'consuming' his body. This emphasises the horror and suffering that Jekyll has endured throughout the novella and encourages the reader to sympathise with him.
  - Throughout the novella, Stevenson appeals to the senses to vividly describe horrifying scenes. For example, when Hyde murders Carew, it is said that Carew's bones were "audibly shattered." The sickening sensory image of bones breaking creates a strong sense of the horrific and brutal nature of Hyde's attack. Stevenson uses a similar technique to describe Jekyll's first transformation into Hyde, stating it caused a "grinding in the bones". The violent, onomatopoeic verb "grinding" allows the reader to almost feel and hear the change taking place, making it seem even more horrifying.

The Characters from 'Dr Jekyll and Mr Hyde'

Now that you've made it through all those questions, I reckon it's time for a well-deserved break. And what better way to unwind than with an amble through *Dr Jekyll and Mr Hyde — The Cartoon*...

Dr Jekyll

Mr Hyde

Mr Utterson

Dr Lanyon

Poole

Mr Enfield

Robert Louis Stevenson's 'Dr Jekyll and Mr Hyde'

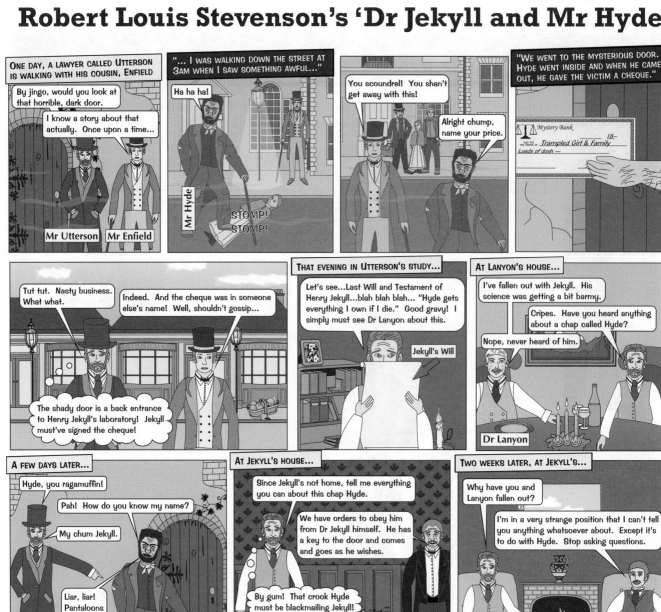

ETWJH41